DS (2)

dreamstories

Also by Kamau Brathwaite

AVAILABLE FROM NEW DIRECTIONS

Ancestors

Black + Blues

MiddlePassages

KAMAU
BRATHWAITE

dreamstories

A NEW DIRECTIONS
PAPERBOOK ORIGINAL

Nuff respec to the editors & publishers of the following journals and a book in which some of the material in DS(2) appears in earlier versions:

'The Black Angel', 'Grease', '4th Traveller', 'DreamHaiti' and 'Salvages' in the Longman (London) edition of Dreamstories; 'Grease' and '4th Traveller' in *Callaloo*; 'My funny Valentine' and 'DreamHaiti' in *Hambone;* and 'Meridiam' as 'Meridian' in *Kunapipi*

Manufactured in the United States of America
First published as a New Directions Paperbook Original (NDP1061) in 2007.
Published simultaneously in Canada by Penguin Books Canada Limited
New Directions Books are printed on acid-free paper.

Library of Congress Cataloging-in-Publication Data

Brathwaite, Kamau, 1930-
DS (2) : dreamstories 2 / Kamau Brathwaite.
p. cm.
"New Directions paperbook original NDP1061."
ISBN-13: 978-0-8112-1693-7 (acid-free paper)
ISBN-10: 0-8112-1693-4 (acid-free paper)
I. Title. II. Title: Dreamstories 2.
PR9230.9.B68D73 2007
811'.54—dc22

2006102893

New Directions Books are published for James Laughlin
by New Directions Publishing Corporation,
80 Eighth Avenue, New York 10011

DS (2)

Contents

for

Sycorax

as i seal these stories. fly their flag of sorceries. w/a new humility

The Professor

for F R and Queenie Leavis

I had heard about him and ha-
(d) read about him. later I reed
his books and hear his lectures
It was such a strange discrep-
ancy . what he said and what
they said he said. Or perhaps
it wasn't so strange after all. si-
nce he defended out his inter-
ests 'stoutly' - had consistently
insisted on values - and the *dis
crimination* of values - one of his
favourite concepts - opening himself up
to a charge of 'prejudice' - *contentious* if
necessary discussion of these *re
valuations* & above all an almos
(t) Puritan - some said Cromwell-
ian - insistence on the responsi-
bility of the artist - and i suppos
(e) intellectual - tho he seldom added
this - for his/her creativity

*(I suspect he didnt really think that 'intellectuals'
- cer-tainly not 'academics' - were 'creative' . and Sylvia
Plath had not yet arr in Cambridge. . .)*

"They" were the people of my
own age - and older people wh
(o) had been like us. happy <<
people. intelligent people. peo-
ple who by failing or refusing
to acquire the *habit & discipline
of discrimination*. nevertheless <
gave off an aura of sense & sen
sibility(!). They accepted 'into
the canon'. they said. anything
that gave them pleasure. that >
pleased them and their *discrim-
inating* tastes And what diversi
ties of pleasure there were!

They expressed this *pleasure* in
tactfully polite & eloquently fa-
shionable ven*ues*. tho unlike <
him. they made no common pur
suit or *scrutiny* of the Xcellent
& Ideal - the Great Tradition

They slept w/no central core of
values and were happy

He was not. In fact I sometime-
(s) wondered if the *others* had
not found the *right path* after all
(with him it was always "He" and <<
"Others"). Perhaps the *core of* val
ues set up too much tension. ma
de too severe demands. distres-
(s)ed too much

But always I came back from <
Downing more sure than ever I
was wrong. "Happy" and "un-
happy" in his contxt had no <
meaning. For him it was only
the fight that mattered . and th
(e) refusal of the temptation to
accept the easy. the obvious. th
(e) investment in the xclusive
& what wd soon be called the
'hegemanic' - fruit(s) of the loom

of Empire - the triumphantalism
of the artist's metaphors down
a long one-way avenue or stree
(t). Against this. for him. there
had to be *choice* - certainly not
the 'one-way'. there had to be
what he kept on calling 'dis-
crimination' - for me an ironic ter
(m) in itself. but I immediately <
understood the concept when
applied to the training of my <
own if then ill-understood 'col-
onial' 'sensibility'

He'd fought - and been gassed -
hence his increasingly terrible cou-
gh? - in the trenches of what th
ey called in England at this ti-
me. the 'Great War' - the First >
World War' - Ypres Ghent the terr-
ible sword&sound of the Somme - tho it
might have been the 'Second' - in whose
dark shadow we are still living - all the
more noticeable coming as I had from the >
sun lit/tle' Caribbean . And this of >>
course was part of his attract-<
ion for me - for us - *practical* <<
criticism as *wisdom*. if you see <<
how i mean. someone who had
on the page reality to *show* for it

And it was true. I realize now.
His method as a critic was <<
based - as after all it shd be - as in
all cases. ideally. these things shd
be - upon his *xperience* - the *open*
ness of having to lay yr life - yr th-
roat itself - on the line of the bayon
et or bullet. and later of course the >>
pen. He been distorted in psych
(e) & lung by these *xperiences* >
from the 'sweet life' of the coun-
tryside - the cottage the crump-
ets the afternoon tea - on whi-
ch so much of the literature of
falaise that paved the way. in
a way. to those wars. had been
constructed. hence now his re
sistance to arms & armies & >>
POWER & propaganda whe-
ther in life or art - *'guns & the >*
gestalt Gestapo' as he angled it in >
something he once wrote . *Blooms*
bury. the *Establishment* - all wer
(e) involve in the *Conspiracy* .

Now he was ready for 'the dic-
tatorship of the popular' - wag-
neristic 'folk' . critical fascism >
(which many of course accused *him* of!) th-
(e) stalinist pogram of the arts
and especially what he called -
parallelling his friend Talmon - *liter-*
ary totalitarianism - which for
him always underpins & in->>
deed menaces the discour/sin >
of it all

Hence his rail against portent
ousness (w/its sense of being pre-
tentiously too FULL) and the <
emphasis on being able to choo
se - and to choose the 'right
way' the right path and of cou-
rse the right *txt(!)* - and how <
not only to read the (right) txt
but to understand - as part of its
rightness - righteousness? - the work's

countervalent direction - its syllab
ically based metaphorical/meta-
physical *intention* - as essenti-
al part of its *meaning* - tho much
of this I only come to understand
after I meet him and get somewhat
to know him. but even then my ?re
al understanding of him and 'the <
whole thing' (as he wd say) only com
(e) much later. long after i wake <
from the dream & parsing of this <
narrative

2
After a lecture I'd ask to meet <
him and he'd given me an app-
ointment for 11:30 the nxt mor-
ning . I was there . as you can
imagine *bright&early* well on ti
me. anxious & curious & sir-<<
teous & undergraduately uncer-
tain of what I wd say/cd say

3
When I arrive at his office he
wasn't there . but the door was
open which at Cambridge mea
ns you cd enter. so I had time
to wander round the room look
ing at the surprisingly few boo
ks on the shelves - but all the
blue *Scrutinys*. it seems. were th
ere and old typewritten lists &
notices on the walls. There wa-
sn't much else. the desk pretty<
well clear(ed) - a few probably
unopened journals a pile of pa-
pers a round chunky young-<<
looking silver clock a fading <
photograph of two people - a <
couple - no doubt *them!* - in bl-
ack 'ole-fashion' bathing suits
shoulder-straps etc - on a blea-
ched-out beach of happier day-
(s) of somewhe that looked like
what I imagined (my limited literary
imagination for you!) to be the Sands
of Dee. . .

The books were well-known <
well-worn standard works no
doubt useful to - *and borrowable* by
- his students - *clearly the library
was elsewhere!* - and the room >>
was small cold bare - more like
a waiting-room than a study

It was. as it turned out. *not* his
study. It was the room he used
for discussions *(tutorials)* with
his junior students. but I was
still surprised & disappointed
at its so purely functional app-
earance

He was late. But as soon as he
came in I realize how even the
bareness of the room the very
lack of comfort was part of the
person of the singleminded pur
suit of his subject . that the <<
room was like a symbol & had
become the afflection of his lon
(g) lonely intensity & painful
implacable honesty. But I had
not xpected this *other*. saving <
quality. his courage

As he came hurrying through>
the door w/quick syntax steps -
his head ahead of his body -
tweedy jacket balden-headed <
open-neck shirt even in this <
early coldering time - apologiz-
ing for his lateness & slipping
off his bicycle clips into his <<
jacket pocket . I was not xpect
ing - since I'd nvr seen him closer
than in the lecture-room - high up
on the bleak Downing podium - ju-
st the Caesar-like bust above the lecter-
(n) - that bright strain in his >
eyes. the tight moist brow of th-
(e) tired anXious over-worked
& dedicated intellectual *padrone*

As he spoke now I cd hear lik
(e) a suffocation in his throat.
as if blood was somehow being
pumped into his voice. and th
ere was some slight white stick
(y)-like rime on his lips - thin.
dry. w/hardly any pinkish. <<
long past the succulence of <<
kissing. . .He looked for a mo-
ment before he sat down. as if
he wd fall. But he pulled up <
his chair behind the spare pol-
ish cedar table-desk w/its rustl-
(e)less surface of white & yell-
ow papers in that waiting-roo
(m) of an office. again like *ac-
cusing* himself for bringing late
yet appearing not at all to noti-
ce my concern and ignoring <
himself altogether. making a jo-
ke about having too many *con-
comicontents* for his age. . .

But when he begin to talk - the
peculiar nasal - the butt of so many
student imitations - as if perhaps <
his very breathing had been scorh-
ed by 'the' *gas* - his high weather-
brown shiny forehead the hair far
back still black Shakespearean <<
domed. his hazel-coloured *thyroidic*
- I know now - emphathatic eyes in a
str-ong fixed tuberant stare . and e-
ven now in this chilly season - the
defiantly ruddy & 'trademark' & >
'season-gnarled open neck - as if>
he wanted to somehow *feel* himself
- *see* himself? - *prove* himself?! -
Lawrentian workman or gardener - at
the new heart of postVictorian lit-
erature - the rest of his body esp
ecially his hands. so strangely
still despite the ruth of thought
thru the words . as if in the >>
concenration & flow of what he >
was saying. he had forgotten >
them -

and I begin to wonder if the <
presentiment of deep physical<
stress - I cdn't yet say *suffering* - I
had had when he first come in
to the room was not an illusion
after all . he seemed now so at
ease - completely the master of>
himself

4

I didn't see him again until a >
year - a little under that - after >>
our meeting - and then it was
very different. it was a balm <
October afternoon. just after lu-
nch. the first leaves falling - a
perfect time to go walking the
Backs. I had taken a path ne-
ar the river . the ground soft <
under me. the grass & especial-
ly the low shrubs wind-glitter-
ing w/a sound of water. the tr-
unks of the birch trees along th
(e) path looking somewhat gr-
ey & cold - no longer silver &
alive - the slim gold leaves thin
ning. so I cd see thru & beyon
(d) them to the Cam - a few <<
people still sitting along the ad
vantage of the banks. reading.
drea(m)ing. trying the finish
To the lighthouse before the ind
ian summer ends . watching th
(e) silence of the punters pass .
. .

and since the path was narr-
ow. the trees and the autumn
weather and the distant presen
ce of the river gave to the mom-
ent that cosy all-aloneness mo-
nody I wanted

I was very much enjoying this
privacy & chillish childish <<
windy solitude. already walk-
ing on dead leaves. when. turn
ing a 'corner' into a clearing. I
come upon him and his wife. <
Both - very close to each other -
were wearing thick brown <<
Marks&Spencer coats - I was st
ill in my eternal Cambridge cordu-
roy - but thats how it was in those day
(s) in that place. I remember - standin
(g) near a large fork chestnut <
tree. They didn't seem to be <<
talking . . . i certainly heard <
the no sound of words in our <
silence. . .

She had her hands deep into <
her coat pockets. her back to <
me. shoulders slightly hunch <
as if she was making a *point* -
though. as I say. there was silence
- me coming so unxpectedly up-
on them. and i was sure that th
ey were. like me. hoping to en-
joy the own company of them-
selves in these delightful autum
(n) woods

He. though looking in my di->
rection had - i soon realized - >>
not (yet) seen me - so i slowed
slowly & then stopped. trying
to see if I cd make myself dis->
appear before he catch sight of
me so really quite close to them
now. for I felt uncomfortably>
like an *intruder* - perhaps. as i<
say. for the same reason(s) th-
at I'd been holding for myself >
just only a moment before

From where I had stopped I <
cd also tell. from the very first
glance. that he had been ill &

my first apprehension of him <
in his waiting-room came back
perhaps had even prepared me
for this like photograph of fore
sight. His high forehead and <
strong stubborn - dashed & dashin
(g) - features in that october <<
woodland light now cast into
his face the shadows of a cav-
ern

This. and the way they stood <
so closely together - *it had been*
them in the fading beach-photo in his
waiting-room! - as if silently supp-
orting each other against pain
& increasing loneliness & *time*
- despite all the lectures & articles
of literary *controversy & triumph* - <
TLS. TIME Magazine etc - leave
me unhotep & embarrass. I felt
- even at my still distance - that I
was leave(s)dropping on a tre-
mendously private quiet & tu->
multuous conversation

But as I made to turn. *get back*
out. he *catch* sight of me. and <
to my great astonishment - for I
didn't think he remember(ed) me! -
waves me over to join them

There was neither eagerness >>
nor weariness in his manner .
tho for some reason I xpected >
one or the other especially sin-
ce I cd feel that he wanted som
(e)how to talk again w/me - if
not he wd hardly have wave me o-
ver - wanted to talk in the way
a vigorous man who has been
ill wants to talk to his friends
& neighbors to convince them
that he's back in his feet again

He introduce me to his wife - <
QD - Queenie - as she turned <
She too had a high forehead <
but it wasn't domed like his I <
thought stupidly but broad . <
her dark greying hair pressing
down & around her head. far-
ming it into a stubborn determi-
ned appearance - his mirror-im
age really

But what made her particular-
ly striking and at the same time
different from him was the str-
ange contrast w/the rest of her
face which was oval rather sa-
llow w/a rather ?sibyline cast -
tho this might have been my own
young romantic imagination - and
ending in a surprisingly girl-<
ish chin & body - the woman
in her. and the wife. to such <
an abstract-seeing abstract-see-
(m)ing person . both lived to-<
gether in her 'slim maturity' - th
(e) very *re*-association of the <
human sensibility he was look-
ing for

We brush damp leaves from un
der of the legba aesculus - he an
(d) I - and we sat &/or propp-<
ed & talked. I asked questions
about little things - young anX-
ieties of future. and little untied
ends that had bothered mwe a-
bout the past term's work. Aus-
ten Lawrence the Metaphysic-
cals his attitude to Eliot but <<
mainly about Lamming in Lam-
ming's poem 'Swans' & the <<
West Indian poetry generally<
I'd presented to him thru a pa-
paper on it that I'd written[*] -
and which he had summarily.<
i thought. 'dis. missed' (it was <
primitively to give him this paper<
that I'd asked for that appointmen
(t) to see him in his waitng room)<
especially since it seemed incr-
easingly clear to me - tho I cdn/t
articulate it then - but glimpsed it -
even as he was handing me back >
my fools/cap onionskin sheets - th-
at the very thing he was dismis
(s) ing from the ?dismissable &
coral Caribbean. was the very<
'thing' that he & *Scrutiny* were
trying to establish here in Cam-
bridge - that there are qualities
& witnesses - thistles . *thisnesses* -
OTHER THAN Received Vic
torianna - which is why i cd <
'reconnize' him at once - from <
the very beginning - even tho -
at that time - he cd nvr have <
overstood - accepted - what i -
and my beginning Caribbean liter-
ature (and culture generally) - repre
sented and cd have offered the
debate. .

*['The nature of West Indian sensibility' -
shamelessly Leavisittian - thot that he'd
have noticed - i thot that might have <<<
helped! its reception! - i was also really <
trying to find out if it was my article - <
which of course was based on all his bear
ings - or our (then early) West Indian poet-
ry that he was 'dismissing' **IT WAS BO
TH!** - and whether - if at all - and how far
i might apply IRONY and above all Lawrence
'(s) 'instinctual' - as oppose to 'civilize' >
'Man' as he saw it - to the Caribbean]

His answers. as always. were
simple principled direct & clea
(r) . but ultimately - I realize this
now - not particularly - indeed
not at all - 'helpful'

[Neither the West Indian literature I had
presented to him in my (unsolicited) paper -
it seemed then such an 'important' moment! - nor my
paper itself - and until my bringing these to
his attention - he - frank/ly! - had heard little
or nothing about West Indian writers or their -
our - our!) poetry - (there wasn't much then anyway!)
- and cdn't - lets face it - find anything abou
(t) it - or my article! - worth serious consider
ation . since for him there was no ***new
bearings*** here - no **rootedness** - no gro-
(w)ing *ground* of culture. as if - *don't you* >>

see! what applied to Prospero didn't instin
(c)tually inclu Caliban

Then we went on to chit-chat.
beer the new ring-road the futu
re of *Scrutiny*(!) even 'the Win
(d) of Change' in Africa. . . >
tho i notice that like his man >

DHL he was more concern w/
the lack of social conscience &
transformation in his own coun-
ty & country - *fair enough!* - than
any-thing-else

He seemed to be so enjoying all
this that he got up - leaving <<
QD under the tree - and began
making little characteristic cir-
cles & paces among the leaves
as he talked - just as he use to
do in Mill Lane when *breaking*
new ground as he call it (tho w/ >
all the ready critics around. one >
had to be careful of images like th-
at in the atmosphere of *Seven Type*
(s) of Ambiguity. . .) We - *he!* - ev-
en went on to dis/*cuss* - *goat*-mou
(t)! - *people* - *'personalities'(!)* - an
(d) *the veX things* his critics >>
had said . and of course *Scruti-*
ny again! and - *'private' as this!* -
his lack of - &/or slow promo-
tion/'recognition' by the Camb-
ridge *Establishment* over the >>
long wars - even tho - and here
was the disclosure which teach me
more than I cd at that time have >
overstood or imagined - *he was the*
same taste & colour as the soil. hav-
ing been born in the Fens and was th-
erefore as native & worthy a Camb-
ridge as anyone cd ever be! - he was
n't no bloody Luddite - *nvr was!*
- nvr cd be! he chuckled - *what-* >
. . ever all that was about. . .

and for once his eyes came out
of their fix far-seeing pharao-
nic glaze and he really *looked* >
at me - w/some amusement in <
his face and a ?strangely hint
of some *relief.* as if - perhaps I <
may be wrong - because I'm a *far-*
eigner? - there was this *toro* in him
- no-way his sensibility of root cd
sense my water - as if I hadn't any! - >
and this - therefore - somehow - >
had free(d) him up - as if it >>
didn't matter - *because perhaps I* >
didn't matter?!!) - and so on to so-
me other anecdote(s) w/in his
albumim

It was so *good* to so so sudden-
ly & unXpectedly *see* the man
behind the manner. a Cantab
undergraduate in those still im-
perial/feudal times . when to >
go to Town you was suppose to
wear yr Gown for fear of the
Bullers & cdn't walk across a
College lawn unless invited to
do so by a Fellow. . .

So for this brief autumn momen
(t) on the Backs am I aware th
at even for this man of rigid di
scipline - this **resonance** so far
beyond my own - there was a >
path still leading back to play-
ful mischievous & yute

But this quick illumination ca-
me also as an added aspirin as

I see the ailing man behind the
txt & discipline. and it seemed
that now he had finish. or so I
thought. his great intellectual >
battle w/the world. he was con
fronting now an even greater <
physical & *metaphysical* fight <
w/in himself -

**How does the trained pr-
ospecting intellect/ual. >
deal w/its *opposite* - mo
(r)tal imagination encom
passing decline of power
(s)lessness - *the waiting-
room* - the autumn eve-
ling even unto the final
chapter of the life. . .**

**is it this *thing* this time
this moment that he *real
ly* wish(ed) to speak ab
out. . .? why when he >>
see me on the threshing
path. he reconnize an >>
beacon mwe? and was >>
perhaps *still tryin to st-
ill tryin to* . . . ?**

He pace those little steps. . . >
walking the sidelines as he call >
it. . .this evening coming w/out
words . . . for we had come. af-
ter the few affectionate xchange di-
(s)closures. to like the cross-<<
woods of the path where there
is almost home. . .oumfô. . .bla-
ck hole. . . and no more woods
. . . and no mo words

5
Miss Queenie standing a little
way off - in her brown coat.
seeming so much a part of the
falling wood. so knew this too.
and in her silence buoyed him
up. So when she sense now th-
at he tiring. she turn to us. sug-
gesting that we take a walk . <
suggesting. not w/word or tone
or gesture. but with her now <
subtle pressure *presence* - if you
know what I mean - that the 'we'
xcluded *me*. The wife & woma
in her had resumed their priv-
acy. . .

6
I don't know how long I re
-main in the fork /of the tree. but I
notice it had started
to drizzle so I decided to take a short
-cut thru the centre
of the woods back to my digs

I hadn't gone more than five minutes' >
walk when I hear a terrible wretching
noise of something tearing body & soul
seam as if from apart each other. w/out
seeing. I know the voice in that coug-
(h). and I cdn't go on. A few more yar
ds and I wd walk to the open air be->
yond the screen of trees that separated
me the person I'd come most to admire
at this now moment of my intellectual
growing up. and i didn't want to see >
him wrecking bent. like that. out here

I stopp(ed)

After the coughing I cd hear his heavy
almost moaning mammal breathing. I <
had not realize he was so far. so near <
I clench my palms and find them clam-
(m)acherry

**Then I hear footsteps. coming
my way down the path. And I
know at once that She was <<
coming back. back down the
path. back back towards the
tree in the clearing. hope/ing
to find me whe they had left
me. to get me help him home
and I&I am stupid helpless . I
push mysore into the bushes
haunt the path just before she
turn the bend and hurry past
beyond me. . .**

**Then there is this silence of <
the waiting room in this autu-
mn wood in Cambridge Engl-
and and along the river and <
the world . only one-one co-<
co raindrop dropping on the<
dying leaves. . .**

*How was he now I wondered . what was he
doing? Had the harsh. hard attack passed
Cd I slip out now perhaps he seems better
and is standing up straight again. and go
on up to him as if I hadn't heard. as if I
didn't know. . . as if i didn't care. . .*

But even as i thought to move i
hear that desolate whimpering
again and i kno now that i cd
not/wd not go. i image him rig-
ht there juss there round the >
corner of my sight. push dow-
(n) on his knees. his ole brow
(n) coat trailing the damp grou
nd his strong face push forever
forward in the paim

From far away it seem i hear >
QD's voice calling - call. ing
my naaman. a note of weary >
hope. a wood-bird-song tinge >
w/regret & pride & defiance &
defence. as woman i know she
wanted help . but as his wife <
to me. i know she wd despise
& hate me if i came. it wd be >
stripping him of all his skin &
dignity association & *naked* in
his clothes. and far more even
more than me she cd not bear >
his bright & broken *telos* - his wor
(d) - tuned to before a help. less
student stranger . admirerer &
murderer . *outsider!* - the *type* >>
who all life long life he'd fight
down to the ground

7

Her feet return . went past my
bide/ing place . and went on >
. . .round the bend. . .

8

in the dark wood it is all silence . the raindrops dripping on the leaves

Cambridge 1954 rev CP March 1999 & NYC May & June 2003. reform 16/17 July + 31 July & rev again 21 Nov 03 & 21 Oct 05/5:10am-9:45am and all afternoon of Oct 27 05 to the usual 3:am in the miggle. kerning
NYC 14 Nov 05

THE BLACK ANGEL

Now that I think back attick

the first time I fee the Black Angel unusual. to say the least was when I went to call on Beta. he hadn't been to work for several days. and the foreman ask me if I'd drop in on him on my way home and see what was the matter. I knock on his shack-shack and when there was no answer. I push open the dark-painted galvanize door and went in. Bee live alone. and as a bachelor. he had only a bed -sitting room & a kitchenette. the Factory Committee nvr allow a single man more

The room was untidy . spots . pans & greasy plates left dirty on the table. in fact. there was a considerable unfinish meal there

he was lying on his bunk. unconscious. his head twisted a little to one side. his eyes open. showing the whites of them

Somebody had wrapt him. apparently. in the Black Angel . it had been place(d) carefully around his shoulders & tocked in under his arms. like a sleeping blanket . there was a faint smell. as of ammonia. in the room

The Black Angel belong to Kapp/o
Kapp/o had join our camp some four months back
he was a dark stocky fellow. w/ a rich shiney moustache
dark hair dark eyes. rather sullen in appearance
tho friendly enough when you get to know him. I'd known
him now for about a month. there was nothing. really
to distinguish him from the rest of the men at the camp. x
-cept the Black Angel . which was his leather jacket

This jacket was a large affair. of faded black leather
. very worn. but warm. which was the important thing
in the cold unfriendly climate around the factory. the cold
grey bleak chill from the wood of beech & evergreens
where we had our camp

the jacket was line w/ a fluffy substance like wool or its
substitute. but was so dirty from long use
that it was practically the same colour as the leather

. I cdn't have said what the original colour had been
. it was a leather jacket very much like what. early in the
20th century. I was to see fighter-pilots & bombing airmen
use

We gave it a name because. in the first place
. it was the only one of its kind in the camp
and we had nvr seen its like. at least so close-up. as it were
. before . and because. when Kapp/o wore it
he kept its high collar sticking up like little ears
or wings around his head
. we use to have some quite heated discussions on whether
the collar more closely resemble wings. or ears. until

someone hit on the idea of the 'Black Angel'. and from then on
evvabody saw the collar(s) as wings. Or perhaps it may have
been the other way around . I can't remember. anyway we all
accepted the name . and in the warped fantastic environment
of our lives. naming & identifying a jacket was one of the less
xtraordinary of our happenings

For instance. none of us had ever *seen* the outer world
. at least we certainly didn't know how near a 'proper' town
was . we were the offspring of lovers convicts the poor
and had been brought to this forest by the Factory Committee

from we born
or. in some cases. from infancy. Many of us were mad
some were idiots and a few suffered from enhystamines hys
-terias vitamin deficiencies & allergies that behave like liars
tubers & blood pressure/diseases . result of the vicious in
-ternal breeding of our impenitential ancestors

And the women in the camp. immune themselves. transported
these diseases to the ducts & hearts. the kidneys the livers
& the lymph tracts of the others of us

Sometimes our doctors switch us on so that we cd watch
our cells divide & multiply on television/tho of course
I didn't come to learn about this prodigal technology
until the day after my birthday on the fist of May

But despite all this. we possess (I know this now)
an xtraordinary innocence of unspoil soul
. and tho we were neurotically sensitive & subject to depress
-ions & profound hallucinations . we possess a moral
integrity & equilibrium. *believe you mwe*

which was quite astonishing . tho I wander still if 'equilib
-rium' is the word I want . since in these 'un
-spoil souls' there seldom was the need for balance
. since the antagonism of temptation. 'the wings of evil'
. were unknown to us

in my then innocence. I was so upset to find Bee
in this sadly fetal condition. that it nvr occurr(ed) to me
to ask how Kapp/o's Angel come to serve him as blanket
in this final fatal illness

II

our only recreation at the camp was boxing. after
work. in the evenings. most of us went over to Gamma's shed
where we did some general skylarkin & a little serious shadow
-boxin

Once or twice a quarter we arrang a more public spectacle
in the form of Championships. *six to nine rounns a bout*

Gamma was a bull-neck. ball-headed buckla of about forty-
five who fancied himself a *duppy conqueror* descendant
of the great & famous Jack-Johnson-the-prize-fighter-&-first
-black-heavyweight-champeen-of-the-world

Certainly his enthusiasm for the game made it impossible
for any able-body yardie in camp to escape his shed for long

One late afternoon. just before dust covered the tiny aura of our lives with its sticky smoke. Kapp/o & myself was walkin down the hill which led from the factory back to our camp. his competitive bout was schedule for the ff night. and he was - rather edge. illy I thought - discussing his chances & his opponent's prowers. none of us ever took these bouts at all serious and I remember vaguely wondering why Kapp/o carry it so diffrent from the rest-of-us. and having thus nebuloosely differentiated Kapp/o from *'the rest-of-us'*. I must have gone on - but only at a subconscious level - to wonder what he was doing here among the 'rest-of-us. . .'

As I've said before we are native here. either brought in in early childhood or *barn-ya.* Yet only three months ago. a grown man. w/a strange outstanding jacket. had appeared among us. And in our *innocent lunacy.* not one of us had initiated the query which I - now talkin to the man and reassuring him as we walk down the hill about his fight - had only now-now dimly form/ulated

Kapp/o usually cycled to town. always he referred to our cam (p) as 'town'. *Going to town?'* he had ask me. catching me up as I walk thru the yard from the factory. It turned out that he had offered his bike that afternoon to Alfie. Alfie had lost a leg a few months before in a factory accident. and even tho he had return to work. he was by no means a ready man. so the use of Kapp/o's bicycle was a helpful turn of fortune for him

At the bottom of the hill were these railings. We had erected them
only recently. to serve as a road-sign & fence. because the hill was
rather steep at this point and people cycling down from a late-shift
at the factory were liable. in the darkness. to run unto the ugly mac
ca 'down-town' ditch at the bottom. So we had all put in overtime at
the factory. making. *w/ the Committee's permission of course* . these rail
ings. modest affairs of cast-iron. and measuring about four feet of >
height after we had stake them into the ground. Later. years&years
later. I am to see these same railings taller in a storie call 'Dream<<
Chad' . But that's past in another storie. . .

Our one ambition now I remember. was one day to make fine deco->
rative heads for them. like in the cemetery. At the moment they re->
remained ashamedly un. attractive & blunt

The trouble. really. was that we couldn't decide on a design for the
heads. Some of us wanted a spear-shape design. like on p48 of 'Sal-
vages' . others a *fleur-de-leaf.* while one man favoured a design of >>>
twine serpents like those at the hospital gates of the factory . so that
by the time Chad arrive here late in that twentieth century storie >>
they was still blunt & undecorated. But we *did* pain them white. whi-
ch is a far-more practical detonation. Now they cd be more clearly
seen in the dark. and did. in fact. prevent many a careless or toxy
rider from crashing into them. reserving him - *yes* - from a more
painful than ending down-in the original ditch. These blunt undeco
rated heads were dangerous

Σome intuition seem to have warn Kapp/o of my then only
half-form infernal queries about him because. before we get
much further down the hill. he had turn the anxieties we had

been discussing a moment before into a joke) himself. became in fact. quite flippant & vigorous. if I can call it that

challenging-me-to-race-im-down-the-hill

We both come laughin panting down. and at the bottom stopp ed. holding on to the now white railings. recovering breath

I don't remember how it started. One of us slap the other on >> the back. I think he was coughing. that was it. the cough catch-up in his chest w/his heaving breath under the heavy clothes he was wearing. I slap him - *yes* - on the back. we. laughin. cough. in . gasp. in all the while He slap me back. My com rade. And before we know whe we are. our hilarious mood leed us. quite serious. but still clearly *in-jest*. to a bare-fisted rehearsal of Gamma's 'pugilistic art' - this weird unaccountable hilarity - *'skylarkin'* - often leading to showers - being another 'normal' feature of the otherworldly climate of our circumstan ces

So there was nothing much in the little scuffle. really. there was no vinegar no anger no intent no ill-will rage. we were both of us about the same height the same build the same weight the same hage. the same level of xperience & proficiency. my > reach was longer but Kapp/o seem to operate on interior lines of shuffle using short jabs & hooks . and at close quarters - >> confine to the narrow space at the bottom of the hill whe the road sharply bend away from the railings - I cd not keep him at my more advantageous range

Soon we were at it quite seriously. grunting & bull-hooking quite outrageously. as if this was an almost future bout. but not yet > sufficiently rouse(d) to xchange brute blunt slug for fine art.

Kapp/o kept his head well & correctly down. his face sink- ing into the high collar of the Black Angel which he was wear- in. so there wasn't much of him I cd hit anyway

The jacket. w/its thick woollen lining. was a soft & pillowy amnesty around his body. so I cdn't make much impression on him there neitha. and I didn't like hammering at his head w/my bare knuck- les . besides. the man was my compañero almost my friend. and I didn't want to humpt him unnecessarily

I don't suppose that Kapp/o wanted to hurt me either. but he certainly was powerful on the short jab and was always find- ing my chin - *don't yu know* - just like regularly tappin at it. tappin at it. each time he hit. I felt my head jerk back thru the universe

The strange thing is that I felt no pain. or rather what I felt when he strike didn't have the sensation of bodily pain. but - and I couldn't understand it - I cd hear myself groaning. In spite of myself I was groaning. But the groans didn't come from my physical self. it seem that each time Kapp/o hit me. he didn't actually hit my chin or my face. but he hit something bright like a star & hard like a hard jewel inside me . my innocence it seem. my spirit or my soul. and that it was this xistence insi- de me that involuntarily groan(ed) & cried-out

i can't say how long it went on like this. i remember struggling ag- ainst him w/ all my will. . . it was my *will* not my physical strength. i discover. that I had to call upon. to use. . .

I remember suddenly struggling against him w/this cortisone & is then that I see that my blows hit not Kapp/o. but like the Black An- gel. it had assume(d) like an enmity all its own. it seem(ed) to have envelope him completely. so that it is not a man at all anymore I >>

fight now. but some Other. w/small sharp black wings opposing me here in the dusk at the bottom of the hill. by the white railings

I felt too that this Other opposing me. was intent on hurting. trying to break. to conk. even to *conquer* me. that if Kapp/o continued to hit me as he was doing. that this Black Angel of our dream - of which he seem to be the agent . *incarnation* - wd wrench me out from the vital contour-consciousness of my body. wd. by this attack upon my pysche & my what felt now like a *sicknesse* in my/of my. will. gain(ed) > an ascendency over and > me. > the wishes of i-self and reason

But then I might have imagine all this . it might have been a merely hallucination. one of those complete acts of imagination to which all of us. as a recompence perhaps for our strangel solitude&situation were so easily subject to. I remember. as in the dream. helplessly. that I begin to lose like sense&consciou-(s)ness. as we use to say *compass-point-direction*. still w/out bein(g) aware of any physical pain. When suddenly I realize that he had stopp . stopp(ed) hittting mwe

I find myself leaning against the railings. shaking my head slowly. wondering what had happen. and see Kapp/o. standing some distance - *really absence* - away from me now. staring back up the now quickly falling dusk on the hill. he seem tense. impatient. as if he was xpecting something or someone to-co me-down-the-hill . as if he had been reading - *this is the only way I can put it* - Lamming's Emigrunts and was *xpecting something to happen...*

He was so pre-occupy that he didn't seem to notice me at all anymore. in fact. no one wd have thot that we had only just broken off from cuffling w/each other

> At that moment Alfie appear at the ›
> top of the hill riding Kapp/o's bicy-
> cle. Perhaps Kapp/o was wondring ›
> what had became of Alfie I thought. ›
> because Alfie had told him that he ››
> wanted to reach home soon after
> dark & we hadn't seen him anywhere
> on the road & Alfie's home was quite
> near here. just round the bend. past
> beyond the railings at the corner.
> anyway Alfie was coming now and my
> silent ruminations must have been
> running current because Kapp/o re-
> lax his*watchful anticipation* - that's
> the way we use to talk in those days. in th
> at place . formal-like like that from read-
> ing late 19th century cheap-edition paper-
> backs - not that the price of the edition(s). I ››››
> learn afterwords. had anything to do w/anything
> like sentencing or style. far less the content of
> its character . tho some of us thought so at the ti-
> me

Alfie come down the hill gathering speed as he came. since he have only one foot in the grave and this was an all-pedal bike . he had taken his good pusher off the pedal. letting the petals spindle & sing their own sweet flower & tune as the bike come coursing down down down the hill

When he is about half-way-down. he see us - always the genial fella-sha - and wave. he also see the white warning rails of our unfinish cast-iron fence and he immediately *clutch-curse* nervous at the brakes so that he cd slow himself for the sharp coming bend & so coast on around past us on to his home in the garden and it was quite amusing to see how his brief Saudi smile of greeting shifted almost instantaneously to anXiety for his brakes

but the brakes didn't hold .
didn't work. It was gettin qui
te dark now but I cd see th-
at his face was registering th
(e) same surprise & fear I fel
(t) w/in me when I realize th
(e) danger he is in. I cd see
the veins of his hands squeez
ing at the useless silver lever
(s) underneath the handle-ba
rs and all this helpless help-
less while I sayin to myself
***how strange how strange* be-**
cause this bike of Kapp/o's
is a new one and since our
factory manufracture them
& nothing else. all of us was
skill mechanics & technician
(s) in this trade if nothing el-
se . and such a thing as >>>
faulty brake was unimmanag-
eable amongst us . be. sides

I was *sure* that Kapp/o's bike
until that moment had been
in the *prefect running* order
you wd *xpec(t)* from a comm
unity of us artisans & all the
while Alfie is comin terrible
down down towards us down
the hill

I was too faze. as they say .
to move - to do anything . an
(d) indeed what cd i have >>
done have done what w/sur-
prise and - now that I think bac
(k) on it - result of that scuffle
w/Kapp/o? . the deep internal
unrecognizing blows it seems
that I had receive. I felt I >>
ought to ac(t) . to do some-
thing to overt this *crash* if I >
cd . but only flashes & like >
skiffles of hallucination flow
over me . *soothin* me and ca-
rryin mwe down like water >
to strange storage riddim cis
terms

And only after Alfie miraculously had jamm im only foot in
to the howling front-wheel-spokes of the careering bike and >>
had given out a cry of pain as the instep of his foot like crack-
out in the dizzy & the whole cycle wobble barely makin the >>
bend of the road like a river & went on still wobbellin & in
pain & on out of sight round the bend to his home in the wild-
erness. is only then that I realize that from where I am stand-
in. that if he had *crash.* he wd have *crash* through me & *smash*
into the blunt naked waitin upright i. ron stalking of the rails

III

One evening soon after these events I arrive home to find
old Mega here. Mega is a pure gypsy. the only *mel
-quíades* not connected w/the factory. tho she spend
most of her time in the camp. She was. I suppose
what our 'cheap editions' call an *ancient hag.* so old
& wither that she look more like a ole man than a wo
-man. I suspect that under her faded yellow speckle
bandana she was quite bald. She came around to our
shack - and had been coming several months before
my birth - my mother's adviser & midwife then - once every month

There is a very real bond of affliction & respect between her->>
self & my mother. Not only did Ta Mega depend on people li
ke my Mo for daily bread & burner (don't think she have a place of her >>
own. juss move from alien to alien - a visiting philosopher & sneer) but my mother >
is bound to her wisdom & her myalistic secrets

She know how to drain fevers. how to revoke bad luck w/flo
wers. and reflect misfortunes back on/to the mirror of enemies.
She cd perdict the future & unravel the various interpredation
(s) of the past. And since the women of our world of mists &
corrugated iron shacks were not blesss w/ the faculty of intern
al mirages & hallucinations (in the same way they were not curse w/our
diseases & neu. roses. tho as I said before. they was carriers of them) they had
resort to spits spirits spells fomentations & potions predict-
ions tellings & foretellings secret hocuspocuses & portions

a Mega is the 'high priestess' of our cult. tho to <<

perdict the future she didn't have resort to spheres & crystals
as I've since seen gypsies at cicatrices do. She simply use(d) <
the large domestic soup tureen. filled it w/ fresh boil water w/<
a golden coin at the bottom - her honorarium. And she cd - sh
(e) claim - carry-out this *'infallible procedure'* only when the <<<
moon was flull

That evening I had come in w/ tire(d) &

nervous from the factory. I had been working over
-time for a week - we were like setting up a pension fund
for Alfie. Ta Mega was sitting on a stool by the fire. coach
-ing my eldest sister Maryse hair

She didn't say anything to me when I came in. but I noticed
that all through my meal - which I was eating very slowly
. my appetite just only half-attending - she had been carefully
tho *surreptitiously* giving me the run-down and as soon
as I had finish eating - pushing my not empty plate away
to show that I was done - she *dispatch* my sisters one & all
to bed. despite the whining protestations of Maryse
that her scalp had not been properly finish scratch

'Leh me see yu hann!'
she begin. wheezing in her professorial ole man voice
as soon as we alone

'Not that hand. dolt. yu heart-hand!'
Always I annoy her w/ my disrespectful *unco-operativeness*
my heretical attitude to the ritual confessional

Now holding my left hand in hers. she long & carefully >

study the tree-lines. appearing uncertain of what she see there
following her index finger alone my palm like a blind ooman

tracing out in her mind a strange new wound on the emboss <
oblongs of her braille. . .

She appeared worried. which was strange. since she had nvr
been - had nvr appeared - worried about me before. *well not really.*
and I had always held this 'good policy' on her part. the care-
ful professional ethnic. *keeping anxious paying clients in a good*
stead of spirits. But this time she *was* worried and genuinely so.
she squeeze my hand so tight against her large discoloured >
rings. it hit me to my eyes

'Open yu shit!' she said grufffly

Now I was *really* surprise! She wanted to *chat* my chest! Ta Me
ga had resort to this supreme act of her negromancy only wh-
en she had *'imitations of catastrophe'.* like if I had *kill* a man or <
was myself to be eaten. or perhaps if I was goin to lose my vir-
ginity or job. But I was innocent of such divine (im)probabilit
ies. Besides. only four months ago Mega had given me the <<
quintennial 'check-up' my mother always insisted on. It cost her
three good golden sovereens. so I suppose that's why it wasnt
annual. But since I was the soul breadwinner in my family - *it*
is my mother who have father(ed) mwe according to Tradition - and the
Factory Committee only employ(ed) women in xceptionella circon-
stances - it was essential that my future be kept clear & open - a
well-kept well-swept lighted passage down the years of my <<
(im)valuable virility

My sisters. poor non-essential darlings. had to be content w/<
two only such xpensive surveys of their future - they were 'ch-
atted' at seven & wd be again at twentyone - if they was not <<
safely marr:ed by then

But as I say . Ta Mega's five-yearly arrangement w/my mother had been successfully & uneventfully carried out only four months before. and here now was Ta Mega. *w/out permission from my mother(!)* on her own initiative. once again assembling the most impressive paraphernalia of her trade

My shirt was off now. and w/her blue mascara stump of pencil which she kept w/in an empty snuff-box at the bottom of her bundle. she begin to draw the lines - the long *horrorscopic lines* - upon my chest

Starting w/my shoulder-blades as base. she quickly construct ed a rough blue rectangle. corresponding to the aureola of my pectors - tho the shape of the completed figure was also determine by the figure of my zodiac - in my case Sagittaurius. lines were then drawn connecting the opposite corners of the rectangle - or rather trapezium. in the > end there wd be a kind of rough pentacle . And the forecast >> rested. it appears. on how near the tips of my breasts were fro-(m) these intersecting lines

Again calculations varied w/the individual & w/his/her astrological mystory. but the principle was simple enough. the state & well-being of yr life was determine(d) by the proximity of the human nipples to these autofficially constructed liminals

Ta Mega is now slowly drawing the final fatal lines of pentacle . she does so carefully. xquisitely but anxiously. w/ less professional & far more *passional* concern than I had ever seem in her before. there was like some foetal river flowing in the place. her anXiety infecting me like scarlet fever. and I didn't have to see her frighten eye to know that both her crossing lines had cross across the staring a-> pple nipples of my chest

I cd feel the pencil passing coldly over & across me like a source

. Ta Mega timbrel .
Her fear was like a heavy stone dropp into silent water.
and the concentric radiations reach over into me
one after one after one

She didn't speak. She hadn't speak a word
after she had told me to undo my shirt

And when she did now speak. she speak
in a gypsy tongue I cd not understand

Deep in the very underwaters of myself I trembled It was as if my spirit was waKing up in the middle of a very dark night. as if I was alone w/out my feet or memory in a wood of presences and powers. vague potentialities & premonitions I cd not see or name

And beyond this wood. moving somewhere around and beyond. A moving gentleness. like the leaves of trees. But between this wind this light. of outer gentleness. were these dark forms and presences. And when they seemed to move. they threw a shadow on my spirit. As a shadow passing over a dark wood darkens the frail trail

My mother now come in. into my coma of dream. into >

my dream of the drama. i suppose yu cd call it. i see her as if fro-(m) a great distance or rather as thru a *'separating medium'*. li-> ke a moving object sheen thru water. she's lookin at me out of a tremendous tremulous distance. like shimmering silence th-ru binoculars. she seem(ed) much less afraid than Mega was

They speak together. head to covered covert head. lookin cross ways at me as if i was some water gecko some object in a pale aquarium lagoon . some object in a showcase of reflection to be looking at

And now my mother leave the room - my other inner self still wa (k)ing up in this new unpeople darkness - and she return w/some thing in her hand that look to me - *my physical eye(s)* still 'work-ing' . tho turn-arounn and like lookin thru the wrong end of a telescope - like a mathemagical protractor - *the celluloid half-circle I had use at school to measure angles.* She handed this to Mega. who (yes) begin (s) to click & measure & remeasure the angle(s) of the mystic-al geographical triangulation she'd drawn across my heart <>

They was simply makin quite shore

then my mother repeated the movemants. made them twice -
like they was makin quite quite sure - and acting so
impersonally now. it seem to me. as if they was gravediggers
finishin off my already settle stuff

And for all I know my body might well have been a grave. I fell inert & heavy as if all time had gone from me. But at the same time my like dying sense xplore(d) the darkness w/a living shoot. calling it onwards. outwards. towards the light & wind of movin gentleness

And beyond the wood of shapeless presences that threaten me. I hear a dream or voice that speak to me of Eye & Eyevil. Eshu singing in my distant stare like a mosquito and & what now seemed Mephistopheles where there was no sun or struggle only this eclipse eclipse. Ta Mega and my mother fighting for my light. only these boulevards of Paris where I have nvr sleep before. only this black scarebird at Saltpond flown in from faar antarctica by a jealous lover. dark & cold. its black spike wings scorch by the meteors of space & left dead & stinkless on my childless footstep doorstep drumstop omen. omen. omen of my even wider wilder vulture future. the dead rats in my alley. the carrion above the breadfruit in my typhoid valley. the sun unrising on the threshold of my threshing floor - no bread no corn no salt no water - and the voices falling falling falling failing from what had once been sun. light

when I recover consciousness it must have been the next day it
was late morning. a pale greenish springtime sun
was shining and it was time for work. No one was about
in our shock. Ta Mega of course was gone
. daylight nvr seem to gree w/her. but there was no sign
of my mother in the yard and my eldest sister who usually
propped up her elbows on the table while I eat breakfast
- it was one of the marks of respect shown to the breadwinning male
that a female of his species family attended him @ meals
even if only perfunctorily as my sister did - wasn't at her post
either. I recalled the fantastic night. the seance. the dark con
-sciousness of evil powers which were striving. unbeknownst
to me. it seems. for purchase over me

Because of this - this curse - it seems my family was - I don't
know why - avoiding me. but they hadn't deserted me
. they wdnt not do that. I knew. unless there was no hope
. and Mega. in the seance had somehow opened up
a channel. Some cornmeal porridge had been left warm
-ing for me by the stove and this I shovelled - *dont eat so fast*
my mother wd have shouted had she been in here
- and set out. almost late. for the factory

I didn't speak to anyone that day. nor the next
. neither at home. nor at work. I develop a headache
. which the noise of machinery
and the spell of the dream course did everything to
aggaravate

IV

On the third day there was a fight at the factory

It was between Kapp/o and a thin nervous yute call Δ
. I don't usually bother about other people quarrels
but somehow I felt drown to this one. I wanted to have
a closer look at Kapp/o in action. remembering the unprece
-dented sensations I had had scuffling w/ him that evening
by the railings at the bottom of the hill

Δ didn't have a chance. really. it was a serious encounter
. both men hot. but Kapp/o working in on his usual interior
lines and keeping close and protected by his jacket. beat Δ
about the mouth & cheekbones until he got his head well up

Δ was one of those brothers too nervous - or lazy - or both - to turn>
up @Gamma's gym

- and having got the lead on the youngster's chin
. Kapp/o simply went to work w/short left jabs & hooks

- he didn't seem to be hitting Δ (too) hard. just going at it
regular regular & firm. but Δ begin to whimper
not as if he was in physical pain - no man fighting wd have
made a noise like that - but it was as if some pressure of
presence was being xerted at the v/roots & feeling his living
& that he was being made a groan like this against his will

*And it was so that the memory of my own xperience. these same gr
oans. come back to me. Δ's psychic pain w/in me reawakening some so
und w/in me like an echo* **I do not want to die** *I hear like in the memor
(y) of a dream my own voice was sayin* **I do not want to die** *And like
<Ta Mega and my mother was telling me these woods & lissening the
leaves of them at the same said time. tho it was Δ somehow I was hea
ring speaking. And a voice replied to a person I cd feel not see . just out
of sight of the dream*

'yu muss revoke them then'

*tho this isn't what was actually said. I am only like translating - and
badly. and at the word* **revoke** *I thought I saw or rather felt a faint
round glowing in the gentleness beyond the shadow of the wood. as if a
sun was out there shining after all*

And a voice - my voice of memory his voice in pain - replied . **How can I . when I don't know how? How can I when I don't know who or what thing to xpec/xpell?'**

And the voice replie . **'I can't say who the person or the presence or the powvr - yet - but I can tell you how'**

at the great word **'HOW'** *it was as if a great brass sound was sou (n)ding in my ears . his ears as if some hand had struck the sun be-yond the dark w/sound*

And the voice continued in my ears/his ears which is what perhaps made me remember them . **'Act by the will not power . act by the will/ beyond yr power. . .'**

at the great word **'WILL'** *the black moon silent sun's eclipse like cracked a bit. hope struck again - beyond the bloodless body of the Kapplo blows - and gold broke forth above the trees in leaves & streams of sound*

V

after a time. under this punishment. Δ didn't fight back. he < had trie some frantic sorties. swinging wild-fisted at K's pro-< tected head. but after each one last ditch effort he had weaken ed precipitately more & more. i wanted to shout - ***and the sun wa***

(s) shining inside me again . beginning to shine through the dark shapes of >
my head - i wanted to shout out to him something like '*remember*
not force. man. not force. but will.Δ . *will!*' but like he cdn't hear be->
cause i cdn't speak and in anycase my words. as *words*. fall >>
chalk & foolish on my tongue

IV

the fellowes who had been watching laugh when Δ fall. the str
ange thing was. they hadn't heard his cries far less the words
inside the dream - or didn't seem to. but this time I was sure.<
there had been an echo of Ta Mega in my mind. And I'm cert-
ain that Δ . when he fought . had had the same deep wrench-
ing xperience that I'd had. And now I thought I knew what it
meant. tho even then I wasn't sure. As I have said before. man
in our condition. subject to neurosis & everyday hallucination
cd be so sure of little . divisions between reality & unreality even <
night&day & day&night - had little definition here

But now I was sure. at that moment. w/an unusual clarity - i <
wd now say *charity* - that the others who had watch the fight had
not heard Δ make those whimpering & unholy sounds becau-
se they - all. all of them - not I - was suffering dreamstories & <<
hallucination

Lookin back on it now. I find this strangely improbable. but I wa-
(s) unfflinchingly convinced of it at that moment in the factory >

w/Δ lying there unconscious on the groan

III

that evening. after my late-shift. I decided to walk round by
Δ 's place. to see how he was. have a chat
and try to confirm my haunch

I knock at his door and when there was no answer. I push open
his heart-painted galvanize door and went in. Δ live alone
and as a bachelor. he had only a bed-sitting room
and a kitchen. the Factory Committee nvr allowed single
man more

the room = untidy . spots spams & greasy plates left dirty
on the table. in fact there was a considerable unfinish meal
in there

Δ was lying on his bunk. unconscious. his head twisted
a little to one side. and his eyes open. showing the blank
white slides of them

he had been wrapt in Kapp/o's Black Angel
it had been place carefully around his shoulders as if
he was cold and tucked-in under his arms like a blanket

there was a faint smell as of ammonia in the air
I smile(d). the generous Kapp/o I thought
. cdn't ever let the other fellow down

Then suddenly I see it . saw it . again . clearly

. the two empty slaves of Kapp/o's leather jacket were really gripp around Δ 's body . the high. two-prong collar like two outrageous wings or ears were like fiX to the youngster's neck

and yet. and yet. of course. who knows. this cd still have been hallucination. . .

The light from the fire threw shadowes in the room but it seem to me. as it had seem to me before. that Kapp/o's jacket was something livving. a fabric inhibited by a dark insidious balance. a living form that was something other than itself

. part

- I was sure now. or as sure as I wd ever be - of the same liver & unseen evil power that I had first become aware of under Ta Mega's spell

I rush to the bunk-bed where Δ lay like so faded-out & silent and tear the Black Angel from the dark moorings of his throat. and lifting it up & off & turning. throw it into the fire

II

when I had held the jacket and lifted it/it was v/heavy and my whole self physical & physic went dark as if I was being cover by a steady shadow or a dark stone. But when I throw away the jacket. the stone was roll away and the great sun come shin ing in/to my now known world like a great gonne

I

when I get home - she was there - again
Ta Mega laugh. not *at* me. juss laugh

My mother. coming thru the door. bring chicken soup
as if it was Xmas Eve or Easter

But high or low. altho I look I look
I can't find poor Kapp/o anywhere to tell im wha had happen
to im jacket

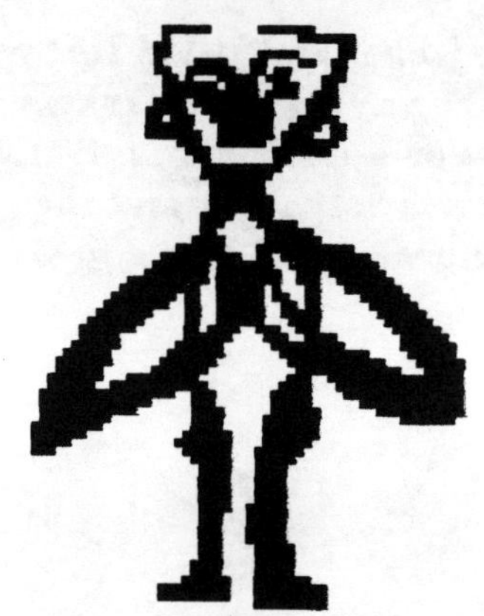

for my Mother
who was writing me this dreamstorie from Barbados 1955 at the same time that i was writing it to her in Paris 1955
Bim 1955. DS 1994. rev NYC rev Sat 8 Feb & 28/29 May/June 2003 . the whole thing reformatt
fe ND into 4/5 w/out memory July 17–19 03 and all over again 20 22 23 Oct 2005
NYC 14 Nov 05

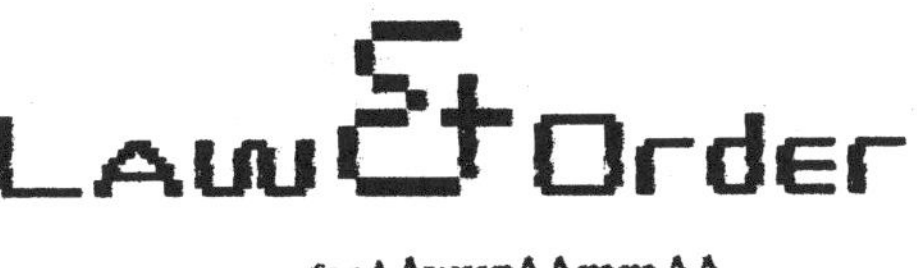

for AAwurAAmmAA

'Let's go down there' Otis said standing on
the road & pointing to the dream. They had
come to the outskirts of the city to the sea. He
wanted to see the ships he had said But now
they had walk to the edge of the city beyond
High Street there were no ships out in the ro-
ads beyond the white shadow of the fort. It
was dark. A fresh wind was blowing. mak-
ing the waves heave in the darkness as they
come up over the reefs. They cd see the roar
of them and hear their white glow But there
was no tang in the air like at Basheba or Sau
tères or even Baltimore or Rockfort in Jamai
ca

Still it wd be pleasant walking along the bea
ch. she thought . even if it was a bit dirty.
and yu nvr know *what* you might step on as
yu walk. Still . . she smiled

When she smiled. her eyes rather small &
wide apart. dimpled & disappeared into two
little twinkles of wickedness. *And she was so
aloof!* So that when she smiled it made him <
uncertain of himself. it made him uncertain
in himself. But she liked him. She liked his
foreignness. his ɔhɔho (what she call(ed)) *eman-
cipation*. the easy *broni* way he took things. th
(e) *amuse* way he walk along her streets. . .>>
sweet. . . that was it. . .w/out *responsibility!*. . >
hold. ing his afroSaxon nose in the *makola*(.)
and the *opete* zongoes. telling her that 'her >>
people' ought to do this or do that . ought to
forum Boards or Committees & *clean the place
down* if the Govvament wdnt or cdnt do it etc
etc etc

And she like that. she liked him. she like hi-
(m) for-what-he-have-for-that. because she >>
know that whatever he say. he was useless. pu
rely *theorem* & use. less. She know he was >>
not *practical*. . . .and therefore . . . she let the >>
wind from the old sea of pirates tingle the hairs of
her armpits as she shruggle her shoulders & smile
to herself that therefore. . .he cdnt be trusted . .
and therefore. . .he cdnt be faithfull. . .

So she smile at him meaning Yes she wd go >
w/him for a walk on the beach. And he. see-
ing her smile. became even more unsure of >>
himself. more unshore in himself. thinking
she was laughing at him. thinking that she
had seen through his little play. his little pl-
oy. thinking she might scorn him just a little
bit little for pretending that he wanted to see
the ships when all he wanted was to have her
have her w/him alone out here on the beach

So when she smile. he was guilty in himself.
But taking his hand. she give him a little tig
of a tug as she leed the way. w/her head bend
& curve from her neck which rose smooth &
erect from her shoulders

She led the way w/her head down - almost to
him like tacit agreement. submission. perhaps the
very sacrifice he wish(ed) she wd be - watching
the path - low straggle-grass-left-over-from-the-
city - that led off the road to the shoreline. It
was a sharp descent this down-to-the-beach &
she was careful of loose stones & loose gravel
& the gutter w/its filthy fish-smiling slime >
that crossed the path at one point

And he was annoye that she shd have taken
the initiative like this. but being just behind
her as she walk. he cd see how her neck flow-
ed into her flowers

Her off-the-shoulder-dress had a deep dip at
the back as if it was made for him! so that th
(e) smooth surface of her skin was like very
close to him & he cd see how her shoulders <<
slope(d) & rounded. and so his eyes descend-
ed to her waist her buttocks the subtile poly-<
rhythmic process of her walking. the cloth of
her dress so much a part of her skin. he cd te-
ll. w/ like a rush of blood to his vision. that >
she had no panties on

What Otis did not realize was that this was
all part of her >*aloof*< Not anything in her as
such - tho there was that too - but just the way
she *was*. . .the way she held her head. high st-
eady & serene & proud. that sail above the si-
pple flowing dress' agitation of her walking
('s) independance. the long seductive image
custom of her woma culture - *àhèné pa nkasa* -
her silent loving loin-beads and *etam* cloth

(2)
When they reach the shore. he was holding >
his nose again. But he did it w/such delight-
ful manners. so am*used* & disapprovingly. as
if he was the clever little critic of her ancient
civilization And she like it All her boyfrenns
were so *seriass*. such come-up-lately Fante po-
liticias & civilsavants & wannabee *panAfricas*

He was *free!* Such a change from her own <
ahemfie people. What a relief to be away from
the warm oppressive intimacy of the family-
circle stools. the dark Kaneshie father's sisters
w/their perpetual *grease-fingered gari* & red >
*palm-oil-*cooking *kelewele* their *yappas* tock be-
tween their knees & *afu yabba* thighs. the gen
erous xplosure of fat suckling breasts. those
brown streak gourds always filled w/futures.
her sisters in&out of the same warm *abusuafo*
room w/their slow motion emotional disclos-
ures & their dark impressionate secrets behin
(d) the warm gold-fingers of their palms. . .
So she liked this irresponsible stranger. <
this talkative inquisitorial into her *awo*. . .

Walking w/him now onto the beach. she felt
flattered & free . even if the beach *was* rather
dirty. . ./And so they came to a heap of like livin
(g) rock(s). huge iron-black slabs piled high and
at random. as if dump(ed) there by ancient elepha
nts long ago but nvr used. piled there perhaps to
make a breakwater. but they'd nvr been organized
There they were now. blocking the path. all law-
less & disorderly. bush now establishing itself out
of the cracks of them. the wild inquisitive life of >
wura weed & thistle now thriving on them. the >>
low tide waves now playing on the animale bul->
warks of them

'Oh' she crie. seeing the water and the way bl-
ock by the rocks. *'Eee'* she shriek as the water
lapp at her feet. She'd remove(d) her 'go-for-
ward-only' sattapatta sandals when they get>
to the sand and the darkwater cold on the to
ss of her toes

So they had to clamber up over the rocks. He
was glad. in a way. Now *he* was leading the <
way. It restored his comfidence. He was the <
young Ɔnanani male again. master. full again
helping her over her painful obstables. . . An-
(d) he was please that she had given in to th-
at tiny little helpless feminine-magazine-li-<
ke *yelp* of self-confession. that small contralto
weakness. He cd forget now her 'aloof' look <
and her sentient smile all the way over from
the ancient Nile. Yes. he was 'out there' again
& she was grateful that he had help(ed) her <
over the flat grey silvery bush & the sharp >>
tunes. . .

(3)
On the other side of the rocks they saw the
full dream stretching out before them glow-
ing w/uncertain phosphorescent drama all th
(e) way over the reefs to the dark cold glassy
waters Calabar and all the way down there. it
seem to the Cape of Hope&Storms Antarctica
and the Southern Star. as if it was a tract of
the watery moon. as if from the brink of its <
dark. it catch & reflect on its strange grey sh-
immmering body. the tidal light & night-mi-
st of the stars

The beach itself sloop slowly up in the wind
from the void voices of the drowned Koro-<
mantin slaves of this coast. their sounds blo-
(w)in in w/ the cold swirl from the sea. curlin
(g)a pall slope along whose top they cd ma-
ke out a mass of beached boats like the smoo-
th backs of large sleeping mammals close to-

gether softly breathing . and beyond them >
the outlines of small buildings. dark hunch-
like shacks build alone the white sand of the
high-tide beach

Confiant now he move her along the loose >>
dry powdery sand towards these outlines He
really didn't want to go walking off into the
long lonely immemorial dark/ness of that >>
hard sea-wash beach - it was too much like >
walking along a snake of where he had per-
ish far too long ago on a curve of the unlight
ed side of another life. Better to have a mark
to move by. and these hulls of haul(ed)-up >>
fishing-boats were comfortable moorings in >
the dark

She herself wd have preferred the pale opan >
beach. The hard naked dream of curving out-
ward to the darkness of Atlantica attracting
her. She wd feel free out there. Here among >
these softly groaning *mpoano* shacks & these
fat warm hulls w/their acrid accra old-fish
shell-fish sea-paint smell she *knew* he wd try
make love to her. ɔdɔ. ɔdɔ. ɔdɔfo

And he did. confidently leaning himself agai
(n)st a boat & drawing her sweet canoe aloof-
ness to him. pulling her boldly by the arm. <
slipping a hand round behind her back wh-
ere the dress made its deep dip so that the sw-
eet natural mixture of her skin was reveal to
him even as she whispered *no no no dabi no not
here* his hands descending to her waist her <<
buttocks. the subtle soft mistoken of her char-
(m)ed resistance

'No' she said again gently 'not here'

'Why' he still askin. ache/ing. like the 'crit-
> ic' he was

The away she speak to him now w/her words
so soft so vaguely artic. ulated. . .as if they <<
were born on her breath and shape(d) by blue
waterstone. only make him *mmenson* & more
triumphantly male. . .

'What's the racket the racket? We're alone <
out here now aren't we?' Indulgent. Fela he <
cd-be. Cd afford to-be. So far from the lights
of the city & the distrustful charcoal eyes of
her mother But she was determine. far more
determine than he knew. . .She relax like for
a moment . xpectant him amourings tightening
around her Then w/a sudden *jerk* & a *backwards*
she free. nur. sing the wrist he had snatch-at
& *lost* . and she was smiling again till her <<
eyes dimple-up disappear into their twin lik-
kle twin/kles of wicked

'Not here' she repeated. decisively now

'So where do you go with a fellow?' he ask >
curiosity killing to know . but too ignorant. >>
young - despite his 'degree' - to be knowing of >
'rooms' & hotels - those still for him distant
xpensive assignations assignments *rendezvou
(s)* 'I kno you don't go for little walks in yr >
woods and they too full of cobras & snakes >>
anyway! An you don't seem to have a single
park in the place!. . .' thinkin of course of London.
. .and sitting on benches & getting her close. . .just the
warm *yeleen* of her dress like between them. . .

She didn't reply. Her silence returning w/th-
at sudden subtle perhaps even (?)sullen *was it*
Af. rican? aloofness. like a turning away of >>
her. self from what he was say. he was sayin

'Paaks too will have secrets too much o'
she said slowly

'So whe can we go xcept ***here****?'* hero's emphasis

She smile his question of ignorence. recallin
her sisters' and her *nenninkumaa*'s whispers. <
the soft *laali* laughter of their seecrets. like th
(e) soft xhalations from trees. their passion-
ate slo(w)ly disclosures. their eyes greetings'
deeper & darker w/ointments & kohl. the ton
es of their gums growing slowly redder & red
(d)er under the years w/the soft subtle kola-
nut chewing away on the indolent indigo ag-
ony of their *sasayeis* & disapp/ointment(s). .

But still she say nothing . placing a heavy
shackle of silence between herself & his quest-
ions. But he press her

'I think it is dangerous' he hear her say agai-
(n) slowly 'for a boy and a girl' - this was her <
language - 'to be out here. alone. like this. on >>
this *iya*. together' . the tip of her tongue soft-
ly touching the little gap in the middle top <
row & tome of her teeth & their whisper

'Dangerous?' His question was high. curling
conquistadourily querulous. mocking. not
yet quixotic but nvr-believing . *broni obroni &*
'civilize' . What a way she bring out the pro-
tective swigger in him! He recover the tiny >
'Eeeee' when the wash of the wave touch her >
toes. . .

Dangerous?'

'Yes. Don't yu kno if the po. lice-dem to-cat-
ch we out here them wd want to mek kas-kas
kasakasa?'

Say' he xploded 'can't you go whe you like >
an do what you like around here?' He was li-
ke Amerika now. *land of the free & the fierce*
. un. democritical & all that! .

'Yu don't know these our po. lice' she conti-
nue(d)

They were walking away from the cluster of <
the love boats' powdery sand back to the firm
open beach by the sea

'Our po. lice here leave by the *twiw* - by the >>
'dash''

'The *dash* ?'

She was smiling. 'What do you say when yu
have to give a man. . . money?'

'Tip?. A tip?'

'No-No. I do not mean a tip'

'Like a bribe! ' as if the sea was xploding

'Yes. . .sort of. . . If you nna *dash* the po. lice>
when they come. they done see you in court
when they go. Yu no see how they stop an >>
man. oova the-mammy-truck-driva-dem? Th
po ignoracious drivas not knowing too much
if dem knock down regulation or not'

'But *whatsthematterwithus!* 'he persisted. the >>
critical wannabee native now. 'What's wrong
with this place! what's wrong with *walkingalo-*
ngthebeachwithagirl!'

'Mmpenda!' altho she knew better. and knew>
how the butter was melting away in his pants
'And sometime' she laugh 'po. lice catch peo-<
ple a-do wha yu juss-try-a-do-juss-now-yu-
a-do. an hitch them up high on un. décent un
less -'

'Un*less*!! unless *what!'*

I cannot tell a lie and When did you last see yr father
The apple fall on the applepie The flag The pledge &
the Stature of Liberty

'Unless. . . they do-something-about-it'

'But the police of all people!' Now he was laff
in her back. shaking his head. 'I can see pim
ps an paroes doin this jitney. But - '

Ah *tsha*. . .she said soffly. *was he really so deep?*
She was getting a little bit tired of this stubb-
born *obroni kwaseasem* . . And in anycase she
had already read Fanon & Richard Wrong's
Notebook(s) of Black/African Power. . .

'But whe is yr Law&Order?' he crie-out. puffin
the toe of his shoe in the white starlit sound

'Whe indeed' she say slowly. sighing x. ass-
piration out through her nostrils

'But suppose the people are marrèd!'

Cd she believe it!

'What wd the police do then?' he beleaguer
the thot that there might well not be 'proper'
Law&Order out here
on this father shore of the dark
quite outrage him

''That song you sing last night'
she say changing the subject. leaning
against him sweet & sudden as Shakespeare

'Teach me that song again'
Her thot like a spear in the star light
before yu become like one of my heavy political frenns

'What song' he say sulky. his face goin blank
w/her switchin the subject. his brain say-
ing *song? song? song? what-song-when-we talkin!*

When he wanted to be obstinate heavy & slo-
(w)ly he cd be v/heavy obstinate & slowly

'The one. . . yu kno. . .'
She was keeping it light. trying to oil an un
-coil im

'The one you was sing- '

'You mean *'Shoo-fly pie?'*

How she laugh. how she laugh. tuning her fa
ce w/the eyes & the teeth white & glow. ing li-
ke the distant reef w/out sound now towards
him. giving him the curve & the long soft sw-
eep of the underside of her neck. The clever <
noonienom-nonsense of the words of the lyric <
like tickle her She cdnt see what he find in <<
'Esse Nana' & the Kofi Nyarku *ablodee* Inde-
pendance highlifes when he have all this jazz
& jitterbogg & what he call *bop*. . . So that th-
eir live. ly love. ly differences now rubb. in <
soffly links against each other's one-another <<
pro. jucin dan. cing chine. ee fire. flies like

Shoo fly pie an apple can dowdy
make yr eyes light up . yr tummy say howdy

II

The seas watch them all the while they walk .
at some places where the reef was stormier
it reared up making its presence felt arresting their attention

so that they had to watch it as they wd have watched some rest-
less spotted leopard in a cage
watch it crouch cry leap stretch hiss & faintly grumble
as its white rage reached the pebbles

nshorë

it whispere nshorë
sweeping over the shingle at incessant tumbelling intervals
& that was what she called it in her language
nsuo nsuo . nshorë: the water(s). the sound of the sea as he kiss her

(2)
Suddenly a tall man appeared on the ridge of
sand above them. close to where they were >>>
walking He was in secular background green
adinkra. workaday not colorful & *kente* royal -
not time&place for that - and yet he wore it royally
And tho the volume of the cloth gave a certain
like suavity to his movements. it did not con-
ceal the powerful swaim & thrusting of his bo-
dy as he came on urgently towards them. toss
ing the loose corner of his cloth's loud cloud
over his bare shoulder in like magnificent af-
lim & omununkum voiolence. the body like foll-
owing itself. the loose & uncoordinating limb-
er limbs increasingly like lumber. that kind >
of proud car(e)less strength that throws itself
about in limbo as if it doesn't notice pain The
loose length & language of the cloth slipping
slipp(ed) again as he came on and toss it back
& toss it back again. back across his shoulder
like a green wave leafing upwards in the wind

He was followed by another man. walking mo
re slowly. almost leisurely. coming down the
white slope of the sand towards them

'Nyena nye kpotoi ani ni nyefio?'

The taller man spoke w/hoarse urgent & un->
<gentle xcitement. even before he quite reach >
where Amma & Otis had stopp

. standin .

'Nke nye baya wolomo le hie konie nye ya dzie nye na!'
He was sure & at the same time rather clum->
sy w/haste as he came towards them. almost >
as if sweating even tho the night was dark an
(d) now becoming cold. His big feet in the cr-
unching cyar-tyre sandals. like flints makin
(g) white flashes in the sand

He came straight on straight on right up to where Awuraaamma >
was. pointing his accusing finger intensely in her face >
and it was as if if if if if >
he did not stop. he wd knock her knock down flat flat as he came >

for a cold cold mom
- ent Otis thot that he wd knock
her down

'Esa ni nye ba wolomo le hie!'
He did not knock her down. but his voice >>>
had this sand & gravel anger in it & he seem
to be on the very crest & verge of tears w/the >
frustration to control himself. It was this pa-
ssion make his movemants so aukward & un-
calm & clumsy

'Yr boyfrenn or something?' Otis murm-
ured. smirking stupid w/the fear he >
feel all over his face . aware of how >
nuseless & *civilice* he feel beside this >
suddenly much larger other. And >>
this other's anger &-what-ever-else-it-
was *- conviction? -* reduce(d) him. made
him feel small(er) & drie(d) up. like
in the DH Lawrence novels he'd been

reading up at Cambridge. *What wd >
'his' FR Leavis have to say about all this*
he had time to wonder. . .

'Esa ni nye ba wolomo le hie!'
the big man repeated. looming like a black i-
conic slab of block. like some thick-skin ele-
phant. like a Bajam breakwater bat. And yet there
was this terrible restraint. like iron His not >
striking as he cd have done was more pain->
ful somehow and impressive painful than a blow>

(3)
When he first rush towards her Amm
(a) had sob a great intake of the Kor
legonnu air. unnerve by the man's su-
dden antagonistic power. But at the >
same time she had sense his awkward
felt his agony restraint. She push(ed)
her body slightly forward at the same
time covering Otis. Meeting the man
'(s) fiery opposition w/a little of her
own. Standing close-in to the wind->>
shadow of his agitation. She was not
going to be *condemn* by him tho she >>
was scared into the very throes of fin-
gers & her towes. So standin slightly
forward towards him she reach(ed) >>
back hopefully then helplessly for O-
tis' hand - not finding him at first . like
someone makin blind circles in the dark.
When she find. . . she squeeze his fin-
gers tightly as she talk

'Mene woyaa fe ye dzen?'
she was saying

Standing close behind her. Otis cd
feel how cold her fingers were gettin

*'Heni wo damo he be wo to ko mbla
ko!'* Steadier now. her voice losing
its high warning pitch of danger
urgency. *'Me-ne he wo sani wo
ya wolomo le hie!'*

She was beginning to be 'rational'

**The man at a disadvantage
pouted in opposition >**

**Her reasoning beginning to
perhaps(?) perplex him**

'What are yu *sayin!'* Otis whisper(ed)
After all this was a *man palava*. But >
he cdn't even understand the languag
(e)

'They're ɔpofoni - *fishermen'* - she whis-
per back the information quickly 'an
they want to take us to their *wolomo* <<
He says that they've just had their *su-
wemo* - their blessing from the wounds <
of the sea - hoping to bring forth sea->
sons - and now we carry-go-bring-co-
me to *tshumuli* - make bedroom - of the >>
plaza'

'Tell him that we marrèd' Otis whisper back again recallin back again the echo of the simple ?logic of his earlier ploy - as if that *namomoni* mattered - and it didn't - even if was true! - which it wasnt - & feelin squeeze & left out foolish

(4)
The other man had come up by this time. >>> shorter. fleshy. facety. more con. genial. w/> discreet intelligent eyes. He also was dress in cloth. mauve *ntama*. but not like his companion in (secular) *adinkra* pattern. When he ar rive (he had come up slowly. softly. like a sailing ship tacking into harbour or like some leisured office of Authority - that in a sense it seems he was) the first big(g)er but now 'junior' fisherman step back >> half-meeting him. They spoke in low tones > briefly. like consultants in the office of each other

'Tell him we *married*' Otis breathe. repeating

'I've told him' she said 'but the sulky says that that's not his cassava. He << says we a-go a *fetish*'

Suddenly compulsively
the great fisher-
man push forward again
making a grann grab for Awurammma

She pull back. not
using a word. the arm of her bracelet
flashing w/fiercely

the one hand groping stretching for her arm her dress her shoulder
tossing his adinkra back up over his bravura

She cd see his eye
(s) clearly in his
like *sightlessness*
the big hard chee
(k)bones under th
(e) skin shinin w/
a kind of half-bli
ne determination
for his
wolomo
& even like a litt-
le stupid & there-
fore dangerous &
angular. His face'
(s) large dark box
like square. frame
<< by the high >>
willfull bones

Otis ignored. still standin w/ <
Awuramma between himself and
the fisherman's danger. made an
(ineffectual) move towards ob
jection & resistance. placing
his two hand protective on his <
girl-friend shoulders

'Eh!Eh!' he begin . tryin to soun
(n) like a native. staring hard
w/ white eyes at the angry It was
a sound of disapproval he pick
up in the Ga Mashie streets & >>
rounn by the Osu NightMarket>
But it was hardly a challenge. It
was far from a challenge. It was
very far from a challenge. She >>
knew that he wasn't 'practical'

(5)
It is the second man who sa
ve the situation. He tugg <
his friend & fellow fisher ba
ck. like remonstrating reas-
onable+familiar. as if speak
ing to a child or casualty . And Awuraa join in. up-taQueen confi-
dence from this unXpecting intervention. til they are all three argu-
ing more 'comfortable' like subtle market interactions coming to a->
greement

Still. it is the big fisherman >
who deliver what appears to >
be the ultimatum. waving gra
andly out towards the reef wh
ere the tide is louder now. he
points out that a certain man>
had come upon himself w/out
himself (his un. himself) endead

&drown (un. fish enfish) &memm
out where *he gesture distance w/*
its sense of threat only too recen
(t) soon - w/its sense of *daakye* - future in
otherwords. his *happening* - his space in time -
cd be 'refound' - rehappen-it again - if certain
tides. . .the po. lice had come to >
make palava in the village. but
no one who had ever seen him
seen - the uture sense conditional again - the
parables of intimate intimidation - wd ever
see him seen again

But what if
the fish shd speak - >
not cd - he said shd - >
and he use the word >
for 'speak' as 'nibble' - >
w/its provenance of >

bait *- of >*
crab *- of >*
dead fish *- of >*
dead flesh *- of >*

intruders on the beach >
people (w/its metonym opete . picker-up >
the vulture) who *defy/defile*
the mananne *- the rituals >*
what wd they not reveal (here again the language moves in whirls in circles tidal indirections)
about this body - his gesturing including Otis >
that will be floating in the water? *The sea-*
birds pick pick pick-up/pick-up/peppers that the sea don't grow >

'The life out there' - now he's pointing to be-
yond the reef - his *adinkra* billowing
prophetic in the wind - *'don't have no mat
nor backdoor'* He pause . letting in again
that black sound of the western catas. tropic sea . and then again
'Esa ni nye be wolomo le hie!' They must go w/him to the *fetish*. . .

(6)
There was a silence after this
The ultimatum rising & fall-
ing between them like the rise
& falling of ***kalunga***. The mist
comin in cold & chilly swirl->
ings from Antarctica

She did not translate anymo-
re for Otis it wd be too danger
ous now too tactless and unki-
nd to Otis for this right now.
she reckon. bringing him - *as
man* - as Stature of Liberty like >
he say - ***and this was another problem -
the Statue - which isn't even a man! -***
into a makola market where o
where she knew he cdn't even>
begin to - to - to - *testicle*

(7)
Not understanding this. Otis felt
left out. He even told himself it
was perhaps a boring dream not
drama. Or that it wasn't happen-
ing And that he'd wake up as if
nothing happening *m'haatha*.<<
Perhaps he ought to take her by
the hand or arm & walk-off from
these people. And yet she knew
he cd not do it. Leaving here >
now. moving off w/out honour. .
besides he wasn't *practical*. and
now had no *face*. . .this business
cd not now be left to sleeping ju-
st like this. Not at this hour. >>
Not w/out its honour. Even in >
the cool damp of Korle Gonno >
night he was sweating and cold
and for the first time wondering
what she thought about him. . . >
stranded out here on this shore. .

III

For some time now since >
the ultimatum AwurAmma
had been looking at the se
cond ɔpofoni. He was sm-
ooth this other. of medium
high w/a soft face soft dar-
(k) skin not fat but 'baby'
fleshy like John Connoe <
the caboceer of Sekondi.
He appeared to take life <
easy. His hair was nicely
parted on the left - a neat <
wide track - Nungua style -
the head well-cut & even -
oily - revealing the soft <<
round shape of his deadly
shining coconut skull fra-
ming the soft round face >
& the rest/less intelligent>
eyes. It was the tidal rest-
less of those eyes & that >>
hint of surf in his half-cre-
scent smile - his always so
ft & quiet teeth of complic-
ity - that betrayed his tra-
der's watery cunning & >>
canoe. his perhaps future
of brutality. even tho the
rounded gestures of his ha
nds were courteous

is he who break the silence
'The fetish charms cost
too much' he started kindly

as if xplaining facts to children
'And it go-make we buy some rum
fe wolomo'

He was the *amankrado* now But the big Other
wanted none of this foolish seaside softness>
With a sudden violent movement. an added >
fluence of his cloth. he shifted his great mass.
averting himself from the *amankrado's* slide >
insinuations

wrapp in his green *adinkra* he stare like pout-
ing out to sea which was flowing in now ris-
ing louder&louder towards hightide. The >>
power of its surging phosphorescence showed
all along the reef of whales of memories of
trade . the dark tight skin over his barter's
cheeks and his forehead faintly somehow cat-
ching the distant light of the water of the >>>
past. horizon stars. even the unseen city in th
(e) dark mirror of his face. He was listening
beyond their talk it seemed. to the accusatio-
(s) of the amuamu this couple had defile

And watching him . what what cd
Orlando Otis Williams think -

oh God! - of *Galilee* -

the lake the sudden superstitious storms - ***alam alarm*** -

of Peter walkin for that moment
on the water - the broken bread
of ghosts beside the sea - the taken token

fish - the miracles -
and he a stranger on that beach - not very far from here

'The fetish charms cost money with this foolish' the *konny*
man was saying. looking hard at Amma w/his meaning

'How much is this' she ask him carefully

'They cost too much' he repeated. wrapp-
ing the information like in a paperpackage in his cloth

'How mush!'

trinket. cajole. cheap costume jewellery

'It cost ten pound'
of flesh
of fish

he said at last more
firmly. formally. kindly and like forgivingly

'They say they take yr five pound let us
go' AwuraAmma say to Otis quickly
not taking her eyes off the Sekondi
watching to see if he understood what she just say to

Otis

'My husband-this-belovèd-miwune-pineapple have only one five pound
enumo she repeated
speaking softly in English-translation-from-Ga
watching him carefully
squeezing Otis' fingers a little bit tighter & then letting go

She and the *amankrado* were like using the same
makola market now . the ritual
of proposal statement silence
the use of Ga-English. Hausa. Coastal-pidgin. zongo-
Hausa. Ewe. Fante-Twi

xpressive vocabulary of the hands
the palms xposed concealed
the fingers stretched refuting challenging e. numerating.
and at last . consideration

'We'll take his pound'

Slow. careful. reluctant. conceding
negotiation of Gethsemane
flash. flesh. white shadow of Columbus
and the slave castles all along this coast

Axim. Ankobra. Takrama. Sekondi. Shama. Komenda Elmina.
CapeCoast. Anomabu. Kormantse. Amoku. Tantum Apam. Senya
Beraku. Accra Accra Accra
Teshie. Prampram. Ada. Keta

▪

So here it was!. the frame-up!

Otis in outrage

As it has been all these years

Otis amaze

a product of those years

Suppose he should refuse!

Otis refuse!

did he in 1490? in 1692? in 1772? in 1955? in 3005?

But how he wish the police
wd come. *now-now. quick*
-ly. some
how . not gum
-slinging cowboy New York
cops dress in darkbubble blue
or black. but some comfort
-able slow-strolling bobby
like the ones in London
Good lord he stutter in his
head. . . *what kind of*
Independence th- th- these people
think they have juss celebreak! -
when there's no no-no law&order
in the place

•

Still. that he had the money. cd >
afford it. reassured him. Always
the fish & the pieces of silver. >>
But they wd have to stoop to ta
ke it! as he felt the crise & fish-
for notes between his fingers. dr-
awing them slowly. carefully out
of his wallet - five only remem-
ber - as it had been at Gorée at >>
Anomabu at Bonny at Calabar at
the mouth of the Congo - and it had
to be the only and the right ones
- thirty dirty cedies-worth of >>
hiss. tory and dis. respect in >
the dark. as it were. as if it was
n't really happening out in the str
eets. down in the dungeons under
Kromantin Castle

while Aramma still talkin. >>
watchin towards the light of >
the bigger man. Otis working
at his *freedom papers* . cleverly
reading them w/his fingers.
the black blank fingertips' <<
desperate *braille*. . . into the bl-
ight of his palm-olive hand.<
surreptitiously treacherously
peering identifying - *he hope!*
- the bloody reddish colour
radish *bribe* of the five-powth-
er cedis until the small petty
successful man. oeuvre ova &
just wow'd him. . . separating
five notes from a fold *& the co*
rrect ones too - first time - in th
(e) dark - and under these cri
sis conditions! it make him >
feel good. it make him feel bet
ter and *yes* almost an*ubis* agai-
(n)

'So. if this is all. we can git now
i guess' The little oneiric critic again. not
so? holding his nose in the masket

(2)
Nobody move because the tendons of the gr-
oup were still controlled by the big tight Kor-
leGonno fisherman. His presence was the >>
Law & Order of their little group. The silenc-
(e) that he kept was like a heavy obstacle &
block beach rock between themselves & mov
(e)ment

He glance towards them in their windy Bight
of Benin huddle & seeing the money change
its hands if not its rat & colour. he toss his cl-
oth back over his then-bare(d) left (or 'souther-
(n') shoulder & suddenly viciously spat

Then folding his arms across the slow high >>
breathing of his anger. he stare(d) again be-
yond their heads out to the restless enigmatic
engine of the beginning of their pain . beyo-
nd the reef . their water-thief . the restless
ocean of their MiddlePassage Watergrate

(3)
Otis
was impress
(ed) perhaps this *kas-kas*
was not so *hocus-pocus* after all

But Connyman was speaking to the *mantse* <
patient now & low & confidential holding >>
out the manganese & colour of the notes un->
certain but endearing out towards him in his
hand. *'They say they sorry and they want to dash you*
this'

(4)
Watching
Otis cd see how
the Tall One wanted none
of this. and he began
to hope he wd not fail. wd not
be persuaded like the rest of
us to this dark fall
and broken trinket box
th *amankrado* offered

Some
-body he repented to him
-self - *shd now be walking on the water*

(5)
Th'*amankrado* was still talking. His small >>
sharp beady teeth were like cold little waves
of words eating their way into the very foun-
dations of the big man's rock as along this >>
slave-trade shore the dark naipaulian waters
of the nightmare break . over the restless reef

The wolomo no-go kno what nobody no go tell him.
countree' He looked at his fellow *}pofoni* kind-
ly. *'They sorry yu kno!'*

'Who *sorry*! Who *sorry*'
Aramma burst out. intercepting the Ga
standing v/erect. her small breasts firm & aggressive towards them
the thin off-the-shoulder *asaawaa* cotton
-dress she was wearing. shining & shimmering & tint
-ing in the whispering sea-light

**'Yu come out hey. don't even knock. an avve *say* howdy
an come tellin we we brek *some* obɔsom when we tell yu
that *is* lie!'**

She know she have them now and cd afford to be bold-out
& *boswé*. besides her pride
demanded that the honours of the frontomfrom
be now fairly & finally decided

**'My *husband says* that if you want the *sika*. yu can keep
it. If not**
- *sucking her teeth now - dangerous like a reef along deep water*
m'kyen - yu can go *an sall* for the po. lice'

Her introduction of ***sail*** - **her use of the word *hyen***
- the sound of the wind in the canvass and the whiff of the sea in her
voice followed by the pebble of *po*
-lice **. the money already red & guilty in the *aman***
-krado **hand -** was wonderfully ***tack*** & timing in their wind

'Po. lice! This no be no po. -
lice palava!'

Then he smile(d)
walking like on the water
'You better be-glad I no let you loose to the presence of the ***wolomo'***

'The *wolomo!* the *wolomo!*
thee fetish no go know wha nobody not go tell dem'
she renammo

'So you better keep the x
-change that yu get & stop this walkin on the nonsense'

•

For the first time the *amankrado* lookin anXi-
ous. igno(r)ing Awuramma - conceding her
contention . if not yet her conscience & hon->
our - he turn again to the Big One. the thoug-
ht that they might well lose the face of their adva-
(n)tage was out-setting him

'Bari. you can see that these people be strangers >>
no? no not the ***shitor***. *the pepper!* ackno(w)ledg-
ing at last Amma's *there-almost-here*. her *mpá-*
ta part of the process. *So is bess we proceess wid*
de sika. . .

The Prophet like shifted his weight once >>>
twice. showing for the first time. small cracks
of what he wasn't certain of. the long line in >
his hands w/out the hauling weight of fish >>
the catch . *mpataa*

Then suddenly he turn. turn(ed) away from>
the story. his head jerk suddenly round fac-
ing the direction he was taking. his big neck
bend round. obedient to intention. the great >
hulk of his shoulders turn. ing . turn. ing. >>
now ship not canoe. the slow now slightly slo
ping body under the great sail of the *adinkra*
following

Bent forward aukwardly stubbornly almost >
like stupid. ly he rush away from them up th
(e) slope away from the wide black night of >
the ocean & back towards the barely black >>
ark outline of the huts & the faint hope of the
distant lights of the city

where only a few midnights before. ShowBhoy Osagyefo Kwame Nkrumah in his <<
Bolgatanga smock & little white triangle 'PG' convict cap had climb the seven steps of
the ablodee platform in the Polo Grounds and in tears had shouted ***'At long last. .***
At long last' *over voices that you cd hardly hear him. . .* ***'The battle has ended***
and this Ghana, our belovéd country. . is free forever. . .' *and the spot*
light show the Union Jack coming down and the Black Star rising. . .and it was so far
away already as if it had nvr happen or happen in dream on this dark xtreme shore
so near and yet so far far now from Kwame saying w/all of us in the crowd unbeliev-<
able w/happy & the shining eyes of pride. . .and Otis one of the brightest among them
in that now distant human ocean since his home island was still only a colony even
tho he felt himself so big-up & cosmopolitan and 'citizen' here 'of the world' w/Amma <
beside him & Nkrumah belting it out in one rapid thunderous sentence that ***'Our in-***
dependence is meaningless unless it is linked up with the total liber-
ation of the African continent' *which somehow until now Otis didnt know*
indou(d)ed him. . .

Then even more unxpectedly the fisherman >
stopp & turn himself back round again. this
great dark clumsy human sailing ship try- >
ing to turn. heaving back towards them. bac-
(k) down the pluff sand to the place where he had stann before >>

But tomorrow - '
he say. intense forefinger warning in Awura's face
his voice hoarse deep&painful w/the roaring sea of anger
that enchain(ed) him

'tomorrow morning. the sun comin up on yr face
esa ni nye be wolomo le hiel'

Then he pause . the silence filling w/the voices of
the millions gone groaning awale awale ye dzeme over there
over the westering reefs

'Yu have to - yu have to come - to the gbatsu'

And there remained in the deep sounding(s)
of his voice. a distant note of whale & desola-
tion remembering all those beaches remember-
ing all these reefs remembering all those gone
i say from Osu Teshie Labadi KorleGonno. .

Then he stoop(ed). his whole body bent awk-
wardly. painfully down towards the tension
of his bending

and scooping some sand from under the two
strangers' feet. takes the *nam* of their footprin
ts

'This for the fetish'
tieing the token sand in an emphatic knot in his *adinkra*

'Tomorrow yu come to th hemfie!'

Then he move off. his violence conceded
leaving him awkward & hungry. his mauve companionion follow-
ing

(6)
'So wha
- what about him?' Otis
finally asked watching them into the silence

'Who? That small one?'

'No' Otis said
Then he started again as if he had trouble swallowing his embarr
-assment & coward

'The one with the - sort of
- well - drama'
the one who was leaving him
empty . w/out blood or *ablodee*

'Tschao!!'
Awur'Amma sigh
as the mist come in again
from the world of the wind & reefs
of kalunga that had lost
him his woman
his independance
his face

'Im only pretendin'

Accra 1955 Bim (Bdos) 1955 rev Kgn June & Nov 1991 . New York Dec 1991 . Kgn Jan 92 . rev again NYU feb & May & June
03 & again reformed & revised for ND 19-22 July & 15-20 Dec 2003 + 4 -9 june 04 . NYC 25 Oct 05
NYC Sunday 6 Nov 05
complete rev Sun-Mon 13-14 Nov 05/3:18am

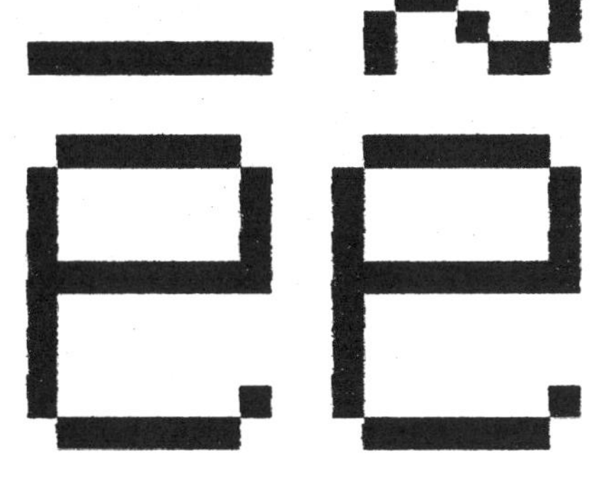

Meridiam

for Frank Dalton at Harvard

ffull moonshine wake me out of my deep sleep

of space
just before 3 in the morning to a blame
-less sky through my window. the BBC still on in the room
& I hear Mora Singh (did i catch her name right?)
giving a chrystal clear picture of a Brittanico-Indian actress'
blues on Meridiam
- she mention Bob Marley in a quiet passion of words
embracing her history & went on. as crystel & clear
as the mid
-night to describe the moment when her parents become
real/real to her & when she. because of this
moved from 'invisible' to visible

She had been awayfromhome - had left home
during a vacation. in fact. against her parents' wishes
- they had wanted her to spend that *'precious time'* with them
but she had gone off with an actors goulp
where for the first time she was able to enjoy a real variety
of parts playing Victorian English. Indian of course
& Calibbeàn
(I think she referrr to a New York performance of a play
by Caryll Phillips) & had retune to find her mother mortally ill

The parents knowing & respecting her commitment
to her art
had not informed her of the fatal illness of their heart
so that she was now back home with the shock of it. holding
feeling & suddenly knowing that this frail woman
- her mother - was not the pale passive sari-wrapt stereotype
failed-immigrant-from-a-stale-wasted-continent-ofmahatmas
-&-maharajahs . three-storied bejewelled elephants . floods
monsons. & thin brown dhoti starveling compleXions
. but that they - for it was both of them - mother
& father that she now be/held

were real brave complexities with their own *com
-parsas* of root. drought. monsoon. bullock. sudden-dust
-storm-of-darkness-nr-Delhi
. cup of prayer in the palm of the wayside fire
& in the time she had left with them. she began to ask them
to tell her - for the first time - about them
-selves& it all came out came out . this new real world
of wonderful people - *who had always been there - not at all* the
face/less sham
/the face/less shame/ful of the schoolbooks who had be/come
her head her heart her fingers' nervous consciousness try

-ing to be invisible to others all those adolescent years
- head down back slooped flingers in the cupboard
of her pockets - trying to be like
- & be like(d) by- *the white bullies of the neighbourhood*
etc etc etc & so *shame* when her mother take her hand
& farward to the playground one-time to face dem down &
all this our own story told & heard year after year after year
generation after generation it seems
w/out cringe w/out change w/out charge w/out hope

even if in differing accents timbres tunes
of the Third World's ios

& yet - perhaps - there was a change - sign - chance - hope
- like the sky through the head of my window
suddenly awake in the eye of the moon

- because
the **BBC = VOICE OF AUTHORITY**
if not of Hopi Indians

but perhaps. though - some sort of Hope
- was '*allowing*' *this*. had read it in manuscript in typescript in
superscript . had checked it out in their editors' rooms with
Mrs Thatcher's mandates pinned to the breasts
of their green baize walls & were sending it out - *transmitting* is
the usual word

- in this criss clear late summer air with only the full moon
watching listening perhaps even waking me up who knows
- to hear what Mora is saying

&

turning my head when the story is done. like at the slowly
end
of a dream. I wished some luck of silver to the lune/
when I see
. in that bright totally royally unxpected clear shining more
brilliant than any loyal cloudless sky - shining in fact *w/out*
any competition of pleiades or other shape of star
that midnight morning full moon

sky so bright so bright no
other beam I say cd shine into my eye

- I see I say - those two
- so bright
- these travellers of light - size of a pin-head - two heads
really - like magnified to the brightness of a stare - two stars
really - side by side - icy volcanoes - e
-ruptured meteors

&so there is this long long brilliantine blaze or tail or trail
behine them in its haze of light. at first of equal length. it
seem
& equal width. quietly quietly humming towards the moon
their double wails of silence streaming back
-wards from their twin-headed un. blinking eye & double
nucleii across the moonlight brightness of the sky
across my August window
my own eye flowing & following across the twenty hundred
thousand miles or more of time until I couldn't see its end
above the roof & blocked-out sky & couldn't get the window
open

-up to look out from its square of dark because it had this
Harvard wire-mesh mesh-in in front its sash of glass
like in the Ancient Mayan Tropicanas

so that you cdnt open it up & push yr head out as you cd
say in Italy or India or in the Caribbean & perhaps even from
the BBC's Broadcasting House in summer - I don't know
- only myself approaching its strange grey rotund sound
from Southampton Row but I cd imagine how it
stretchwaayacross my skin how many many miles& more

&so I decided that when Meridiam done - & they were now
talkin about *xperimental work in ∂rama at this year's E∂inburgh*
('Edinburough'. 'Edinboro')*Festival*

es. pecially an Italian director's *Macbeth* which had been
produce in like three living volumes - venues
- then somewhere else - can't remember where because my
mind
was now so torn by now by the sky & the happenings
up there - all that bright
wind &wandering how many people were seeing at it this
time of summer midnight sky

&

I guess that by now some man
-drake muss have phone the police
& the newspapers - *someone always seems to pho the polizei*
e3 klook klook klook klook klook in the sky
- you can't miss its long swift blowing desert by the moon

& there was like this spike & spearhead of light just behine
that double star & helix pointing at the moon

so

that while Meridiam still on & talkin about the third
venue - an island in the Firth or Froth of Forth
I think it was. & how the vision of the Bridge - over the Firth
- isn't this one of the great bridges of the world?
of the Industrial Revolution? of the Modem World?
- tho not part of the scenaria

- was somehow like part of it - the play - the theatre - in
-corporated into the very Festival's Palatinate & Palatino celebration of
Shakespeare's *Ecosse.* the very coast & cost of the island itself somewhere
out there beyond even the star-cross wave
-lengths of the BBC . *whe the Norweyan banners flout the sky*

&whe the water must have been very very cold. murky even
. from the '*dour colour of the stone*' out of which it comets
. spawning brown hookmouth trout & Nessies
welcoming us with fires on the water - like memories
against the glaze & avalanches of the Ice Age - the fires
burning on the radio of the water & along the water's edge with Verdi's
Requiem & versions of the play
- the commentator was saying
- & all against the background - back
-drop. really - of a '*fantastic northern sunset*'

& all against the frontdoor/window of these meteors across the
foreground of my forehead & how one trail was shorter now &
fainter & less broad. er than was the other - *or is it my i.magination*
- no - one trail or tail is shorter now. more 'junior-like' - or so
it seemed - tho both = they kept their equal diamant

&with the woden quadrants of my window. I cd judge how fa
st how fast they movin - though you know how it is with thing
(s) in the sky even aeroplanes in certain places certain times <
seem to fly in the same pace forever. &of course. at first. when
I open my eyes & see the sky. it was a plane - no - two planes - >
flying there near&next to each other. sidebyside with two whi-
te navigation or warm. ing lights on. bright & probably going
in to land at Logan Airport with their two long slipstreams be
hind them even at this time of cold & colour in the sky & I'm
listening for the sound of their engines though at that height
you probably wdnt hear them & at that eagle & as I said. they
seemed to be moving so slowly that it seem sometime they did
n't move at all &why were they soclose togather - *that was very
unusual xcept for the showing-off sessions at airshows* - & it is only
then that I realize - recognize - that these were no airlines but
what the sky-fi books call '*interplanetary visitors*' - which perha-
ps is why they are so bright so swift & seemingly unmovingly
together - two very near & distant planets or 'planetary bodie-
(s)' moving at terrrific rush through space ¬ towards the >
Logan Airport but the moon

& I could see that - see them - feel them - almost hear them -<
gauging. as i say. their curve of movement from the wooden <
quadrants of my window & I was getting anxious to get up get
out out of bed out of the warm & dream of the room & be out-
side on the side/walk & into the red world. as it were. so that I
could look up at like the real/sky. not just the sky through the
head of my window & I know I cdn't go on listening & listenin
(g) to Meridiam tho I wasn't really listening & cd see from th-
(e) square little black watch that I kept waiting by my bed nea
(r) the radio that it was still

four
minutes to go before
3:00
in the morning before Meridiam done

but suppose something happen before that
like the '*phenomenon*' stop - tho I didn't think. from my
xperience. that sidereal (asdistinctfromsurrealist) events. taking
place so many millions
of lightyearsaway. hardly ever suddenly **stop**
as easily as brakes

say. or balancing acts or castles of cards in the air
- I mean it was not like a cracker or the carnival
at Carnavaral
or star/lights you hold in November fingers
their sharp little flick
-ers of diamond teeth snapp/ing like harm
-less against your feast

&

yet - yet - you cdn't be sure
I mean you cd imagine the mmmmmmmmmm & speeeeeeed
of the limitless power of these star-wars perhaps even star
-weary meters of light enter/ing into the land/
scape of our continent

but there wasn't any tick there/there wasn't any noise
or quantum in their engines
& that. I realize. was the difference between 'earthly things' or
'*lingo*' like the black digital beside my bed

& 'things in other dimensions' like fish in their author
or listening to dreams or watching this double-headed all-lit
-up 'heavenly body' rushing towards the floodlid lands
of the clouds around the Harvard

moon

& why am I using all these big words like sidereal
& quotidian & surrealist &

quinquenoctial

which I don't evenknow in the dream & can't even spell &
I mean what's going

ohnnn

because normally when you see the moon you wish & wonder
if your loved one or loved ones are seeing it two &
when I open my eye from the dream I think of you

but as soon as I see these space-wrecked glaciers
it is as if it's a private show & something confine to the sky
of my room & I wonder why be/cause if the moon cd be seen

all

over the world & that same moon had been seen
even before by people in India & Bangladesh & the BBC
or wherever the smmmmm come from before it reaches us
from over the horizon of time/zones or what/ever

then surely all over the world they would be seeing these
meteors too or hearing them in their hearts or hotels
But we it seems - have nvr been able to share comets
or meteors or shooting stars - not even
aurora borealis - or the same sun for that matter - x
-cept in eclipse
- or in 'temperate zones' in 'very good weather'
- when you come
to think of it - in the way we share the moon

but these meteors these other outer uttar visitors & cultures
these realystrangers - perhaps even dagger or dang. ers - as in
Macbeth - xcitements unexpected too silently intense to share

something perhaps to do with the heavens - or heaven - & how
it takes us out of the our slaves - I don't really know or under-
stand - but I know that I was getting increasingly impatient
with Meridian for

not finishing - as if Time wd nvr come to
its end
- & - yes - I begin to worry - despite my earlier ?cool
and what after all - suppose if the meteors finish before
Meridiam done!

They had like appear so easi-

**ly out of my sleep & there had b-
een no war or warning about th-
em not even a whisp or warship
of prediction upon the cloudless
weather forecasts tho as soon as
I had open my eyes to the moon I
remember one guy - don't ask me wh
(y) - a slim brownskinnish smiling
TV weatherman - tho all wither-
people on TV (can't remember seeing a wo
man in any of these dreamss) seem reQuire
(d) - or were reQuested - certainly
determine(d) - to smile. to be** *ha-
ppy.* **to be up-beat -** *up-market* **as
they sayin now inna these days
& some carry-on carry-on as if th
ey was maniax**

**& I remember this fore/caster or
ncashier not because of his cast
but because he was the one who
quipp-back-fass to one of his (wh-
ite) colleagues on one of the Net-
work(s) who was tryin a ting - on
(e) of those lime-lame improvize
jokes at the end of the Nose. no?**

it was like

8.8.88

one of these special moments in the world of time esp since it was also eight minutes pass eight the day Fergie daughter wa (s) born & the (white) NorthAmericans as usual had gone ga-

ga (*Queen Time People Enquierer* & all the networks etc etc etc) & was giving 'The Royal Event' as much airline as baseball or anti-tartar > toothpaste & they had proudly pronounce her name

- MARY ELIZABETH BEATRICE ALEXANDRIA -

'a whole long dynasty of forebearers' & how after all that (this guy seh - fornogoodreasonatall) she wd prob be known as 'B' & this cl-own was saying - in like the black&white days long before Princess Dianna Death & the Monica Lewinsky Scandal & the Presidential Impeachmemt & 9/11 & of course not Tourists anymore but TERRORISTES - that if she was a good little girl & become granny's pet she might one day become

QUEEN B

GET IT?

QUEEN B?

QUEEN BEE?

when our brownskinnyguy (known of course in the Books - nomatter whatNetworkorTetrarch he was on - as a 'Negro') come right back **bax** w/out black(s)-in-u-eye as it were - **with**

ONLY

A WASP

COULD SAY SOMETHING LIKE THAT

(get that one two? whatever dat mean when dog eatin dawg)

so no wonder I remember this guy &im forecast a few weeks ago about A Big Bermuda High & Full Moon Tonight
etc etc etc

- *but no hint of comets* -

so that - who knows - I was perhaps witnessing something out
of the xtraordinary & I almost switch on the radio - the one in
my livingroom/workingroom/wakingroom - not the one nxt
to the bed that was still playing Meridiam

- to see if they was any news - tho the media. I notice. with per
-haps the *solaris* xception of Awesome Welles &
some of the builders of the

- pyr^A^mids -

hardly ever cotch up with anything out of the ☼ until well aft-
er the Event -

unless of cost they had themselves perdicted it or publicized it
- like an eclipse or the alphabets of hurricanes or Haley's (Halley's) Comet

& so I thought I better get up & put on some clothers & get out
& see for meself since I didn't want to miss what/ever was real
ly happening out of the xtraordinary high up above the case-
ment of my house

& in anycase. I say to myself. why shd I be giving priority to
something inside the radio or radar of my head when somethi
ng 'raw' is happening outside in the sky - or was it outside of
the sky - & I cdn't really lie waitin & waitin for the last four <
minutes of Meridiam to finish when I wasn't even listenin & I
cd dress in the meantime & in the end I didn't even hear the <<
end of the programme even tho from like the corner of my ears

I cd hear them going on about jazz & jazz festivals & matchin
or marching bands like in Norleans tho this was still the Ed-<

inborough Festival & as I was leaving the apartment I hear th-
em sayin that after the News they was going to be some more <
music this time some Indian music no not by Ravi Shankar<<
but by a nam beginning like *Shif*

but as the BBC's General Overseas Service seem to enjoy
saying
to we lout here in the colonies - just when we gettin intrested
& settlin down into what they doin so well - let me tell yu
dat!

- tho by this time I had stoop listening even tho I had been
tryin
- as you must have notice - to do both things at once
& the sametime
& there must be a moral or miracle in here somewhere

**THIS TRANSMISSION IS NOW CLOSING. . .LISTENERS
. . . IN AUSTRALASIA . . .**

where I am sure there are many - don't their flags have plenty
stars in their sky & not crowded & set out in order
-ly mewes like in the United States of America
- shd now turn
or tune to so many thousand megahertz

& at one time I use to try to see if I cd get these palaces on that
same little computerize Sony I had been listening Meridiam
on
. but nothing ever come out but the static I suppose
of Australasian stars & by now I was thru the door & down the
steps & down
the steps & thru the street door & back down onto the earth
of the pavement in front & below my apart/ment

& I look up at the parch
-ment of the sky & see nothing nothing nothing
but swirling clouds like
on Creation

Morning & so I thought that it must be over the housees
especially since the night was getting like cloudy okay?
so I cross over to the other Nile

of the street - I suppose it was - tho I can't be sure anymore
& there was nothing there neither - neither moon nor sizzling stars
as if they had swallow each other

& it was only then that I kno that when I had first come
out of the house & look anxiously up from the somewhat
unsteady feet of the pavement x/pecting to see all that light
- the wonder of comets of the early morning

- the miles & miles
of its trail across a sky so whitened & brilliant
it cd makeyoubline

that I had seen like between myself & the sky like an empty
pool. dryly & like drably jutting out of my dream as I cross
slowly back to my side of the pavement. my flat face staring
up in. to the dark empty space - no - *yes* - I hadn't been wrong

- of a flagpole
- a long steel metal flagpool jutting out from the front
of the apartment above me - above mine - had nvr notice it
before - but the building apposite had one too & on the 4th
of July I had seen an ever patriotic - even dutiful
- *Stars&Stripes* drape proudly\ & flying from it - nxt
to the doll of a small naked legba or girl
that some lampooning lamposting student had guillotine
there on that crossroads of space. climbing & clambering
outer & onto his life & his limbo. it seems. to achieve

& it was only then that I began to confirm - in a way I began
to con. form - that that whole night through. rused
from my dreams by the now absent moon

I had been looking at light thrown onto the sky
not from the whisper of plumets that had opened my eyes
not even from radio fires on the distant island of Skye

but from the everyday light of the everynight streets relflected upon
that flag-pole of white/steel & that that everyday light. catching the
tips of the pool had created those close two gemini stares

in my head & that that short thinner staple behind them
had burnish
the speartip of light

& that the main body & shaft of that banner of night. in -dented &
cleft along its long length like the balancing muscles or scales on either
side of your spine

were the two simple ropes of the halyard dividing itself
in the sky into that doubling stream of the snake

of the universe flowing with counterless stars
towards the black hole of the moom

& yet as I sit here this morning tryin to wrestle these words ba ck to dream . I look across at there isn't a doll at the end of that halyard not even a pool or a flagpole jutting out from the night of the building . only a red rusty bracket or crayfish of metal w/a large caterpillar or little dead tadpole or flesh playing down from its fetish or totem

on a slowly dwindling wire or sing as if I had witness
a midnight Meridiam
too crowded too distant too tundra & cowl & too glitter & cold
- for any memo or saving or sense of what we call caritas - charity -

love

as I

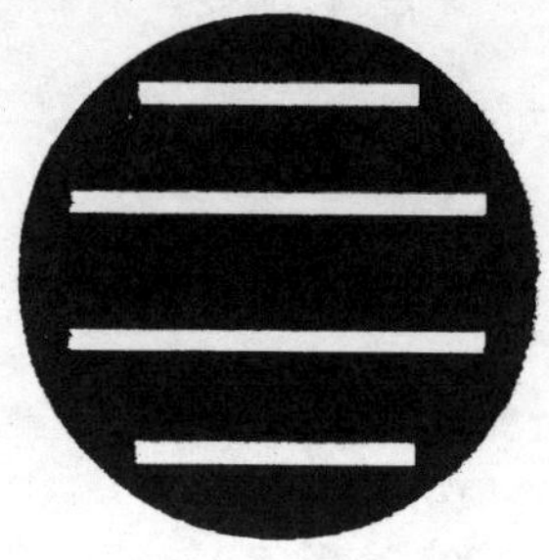

-                                   -

pen my eye from the deep sleep of space & hear in
the silence that follows the rain or the passage of
stars or Meridiam pain .
Shif Kumar Sharma & HariPersad Charvarsia .
praying their morning raga

grease

for Jere

T he water of the mirror in the room is dark

greem
quiet as translucence in the light of a limestone cave
nr the ocean
and it had been pasted on/to the wall like a map
the shape
of a ilann . one of those lopp-
slidèd half-square Caribbean-shape ones like
Trinidad or central

Virgin Gorda

bicycles of clock bangg from the sky of the ceiling
& there was a large black snortless hunchback motor-
bike yu wd hardly notice like some large stuff
animal or dead watchdog in the coroner

It was the plumber's shop or place of business & his tools -
compressor. steel rods. borer. corkscrew. plunger

- pit-block. snake-bolt. witch-hazel-ariel -
was grey spinache-colour fossils or dead aborted insects

of all shapes & snizes
lying like asleep in boxes. on dirty botched-up
butchered tables even uncrawling on the floor

he plumber himself is like a pearson

walking in dead
grass that was dried grease

stale stain stencils of yesterdays black spaces
printing their patterns on his now almost invisible
garment of cloth skin leather flesh of old
newspaper(s). and his large bright hands were like
smooth blind eyes which he held out before
him like a hearing aid that he use as a searchlight
into the pits

& pus & refuse & the soft black starch of latrines
. the black slag
of the ten thousand hours of how she use to sit
w/ her eyes straining close(d) in the darkness of her
priv-

vvvy which was now as public as the multi. cultural
flags of sheets
& trousers & coloured
shirts left hanging from their wrists on the bleach
yvvvvvy clotheslines yvvvvvy

of the ungo V ern. mental
yard that told the blue curled flapping morning
world
that the goodwife was at home. cooking w/ clean
wipe hands

minutes of soapsuds ticking up to her elbows
sometimes. flogging them off onto the squared
crook/ed floorboards pee. ling off
the flowery fields of linoleum & sticky to her bare
feet & so

slightly musty after the mop. looking down at her
feet far below
the blue apron w/out suc. cess. soiled fence against
dishwater & evil droppings of surcease. not even
against the tell tale trail
of the mice . saying aloud

since there was no one to hear or inferr that the
water runnin too slow-
ly today in the grey day now grasping for breath in
the kit. chen leaning over the sink
& straightening up so she wd not sink down
the steep purring gulch of the mem-
ories of more roaches then she cd ever have handle

the brass
tourniquet of water that turn
them off. overflowing like ants really. tick-
in like a large ugly wristwatch of death
under her very window. un-
der the concrete slab that covered her privacy
now the business not now of the plumber. her

husband. but this sly false schlooslt keymaker who
had enter her life thru a gimlet
as it
were. when all the locks shd have been shut like her
eyes against in. vasion & the hand of war. but

she had seen him pee-
pin in at her w/ his two long thin antennae
searchlight eyes
thru the blind open breathe of her window-curtains
that she shd have been washin for Easter

but hadnt because of the ru. mour of earthquake
. the heat so early
in the year already like a tumour she cd feel
. sometimes see
like a soft grey mist weaving behind her sight

on the right-hand side of the road she walked
from the supermarket w/ the
indenture blank of her face
forcing her eyes to see thru their pane
as he. squint. in at her thru her key-
hole was seeing her now
as if for the first time. which

he was. which
he was. thru the thousand silences of the dresses
she had nvr
been able to buy. to off. ford. to wear. to share
w/ the boys who wish so much to strip

her of the village
she had nvr forgotten even tho she had come to
town
so many footnights before on the bar of her fathers
bicycle &
they had gone to live behine the lawn-

dry mat next to the Chinese grocery shop
in Mallimes before she had gone fishing one early
morning off the Palisade Road w/ that plumber
watching the pink light of si. lence come up over the
graveyard & the casuarinas &
the long mountain still sleeping like a huge grey

iguana.

by Wareika & Rockfort . the side to her still quick
tho quiet
like how rabbits are when they appear
to be sleeping w/ just that little twitch of the ear or
the fear of their fur like a flicker of memory nostrils
not like the rats she had seen comin out of the slink-
whole & there was like pink in the grey water where
she stann
in her gunboat socks. his bare toes become crabs
afraid to be lobsters

& a fish come up quiet as toothpaste out of its tube
of water on that line in im hann before they went
home to the new kettle. its breath warm on her back
when she turn her back to it in their small crowded
submarine room & he duckin his head down a bit

combing his hair in the mirror & lookin at his
himself w/ a little
half-lighted admiral smile. making sure that he
still had a face. as it were. and lingering over the
memory of the pink

morning w/ the fish of his feet in the socket of water
as the eye of the concrete lid was clanked up over
his grave
by the hearing aid of his hands that shd have been
wearing gloves when he kiss(ed) her

ut there was so much pollution now

in his heart
these darkening frills of water filling the shoreline
w/ man. grove w/ the slow black lips of what all
those ships & fats & fact-
ories had voided onto the shore of what shd have
been white sand already browning when he was

growing up. coming over the hill
by the cement factory to this wide green ripple
breathing the space of silence that was once
the greatest admiration harbour in the world
flags of all cartons flying. duck. duke. drake.
benbow. karate morgan. rodney. blood-
red half nelson. rear admiral girvan. commander
patterson unfathomable pollard. flag-
waving captain carlos campbell. *what can I tell you?*
his little flinger flying in the air
paddle. sail. stale steam. piddle of voyeurs

o voyageurs

collusion of bauxite liners where she had once
smiled . her breasts bare dunes their slopes slip
slipp. ing soft. ly down as he sat. before the days
of gunmen. by that box in the yard under the
tamarind tree w/ its green dripping leaflets & brown
acid-drop-pods that crack
in the char cool coal of yr cannon hands when

they are ready. that make yr mouth water. fine
tuning the stations of the cross to hear the first cold
thirsty christ of the andes. the sand now slippering
down the crystal tunes of her tundra. the thundra
now entering their lives while her kettle song sing
a clear silver stream of saddam that was like a genie
of escape from all

that grease

& the worms under the lids of the skillets of his eyes
that he wd hang up on the nail behind the door w/
his trousers when he came in from wreck late
in the afternoon or evening. depending on the

wrock

on how much overtime he had been able to 'secure'
for always spoke he like that
as if his work was something to protect or guard
like a dog
or a bank-roll or a milk
that yu wanted to drink flesh-fresh from the files
or a black rock

which in a sense was the case
since they depended on each pail & penny that he
got . or like when he had been out w/ the boys or one
of his lavender women as she call them

which went on rattling at her. esp when he was
speak. *ing at her. at her. at her*
as he had started to do from the nail of the
afternoon coffin
of his clothes. now that they had move away from
her mother

into this ungovernmental yard in the Gardens
where all the women had rims of real gold in their
noses & sometimes zodiacs
of brilliant palmtree cargo swaying from their ears
& flashing tempers

& he was like plumbing for her runes & roaches
even as
he banged her banged her banged her
on the flat concrete slab of their agony. the mist
of his breath & the moist of their effort & anxiety.
for it was surely

this she had come to recognize
in the always labouring labouring labouring man
that fall upon her dreams like the sweatprints
of a ship of war. its tar. slack. slag

sticky tomorrows of gunfire & fuck in the
Persian Gulf where Moses had startled the Red
Sea w/ his stick of snakes so many charioteers ago

.

the sorrows upon sorrows swimming across the
row upon row
of the words of her Bible . the long dark stretched-
out sleeping deck now of her husband gulping &
snoring his nose & ignorant & ig. noring. like the
sound of ships passing thru the Straits of Formose

or she had nvr in her wildest

as she tell mwe later in the dream. xpected that this
loving & love-vine entwining cd have become so
yellow & entangling. she tryin
to trample out of his contaminating reaches. his
hand like an unbless tonsure or wound in the tight
knitted thighs of her canerow or cornrow . the ache
in her hair like the pink dawn coming up over the
mountains

of eddoe(s) & aloe vera & sighs
even tho she was closing her eyes to all that light
of the charity

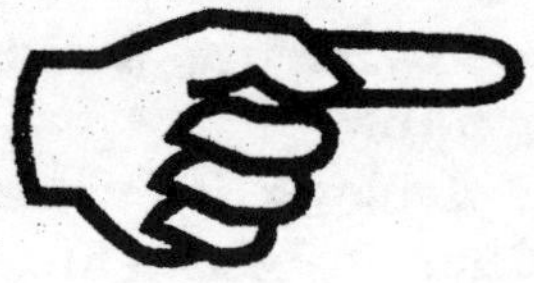

or all before she had known

of plumbering
it had been soft - yes - and gentle trampoline as she
had read
in mills & other blooms of books w/ their fine
neutered nvr nervous sense of elvira & the S
of France & the grapevine(s) growing
so close to the house

. it was like. it was like. *loyalty & hymn books*
& sunday services since she didn't know France
nor any of those palaces
& might nvr reach Cayman or Chaguaramas
not to mention Miami the way things were not going
tho there

had always been rebellion against all the signs
this cosy & comfort in her not always choosing. as
she put it months later into the purse that her
mouth had become. to close

the knees of her eyes before the parson's long mix
metaphor
-ical arm of the sermon be
-gan & refusing the batter & blood & worm-down
coigns of his body

S_o

that when she see this gimlet man. his braun polyester
zip-up jacket. so diff rent from the swan she see out-up in
Chapelton Gardens. this car. penter not plumber. w/th-
is look thru her dress right into her womb. as it were .
cur. tains & chintz. as if. yu kno . she was a window or
widow. something like that is-how he make her feel .
navel & naked & needing

S_o

xpose that she swim away her eyes from his eyes but still
lettin him see see see see it all. really. like if she cyaaan st
op sheself she cyaaaan help-it. right-thru these clean lace
curtains of comfort into the rats & the roaches & grease
of her cesspit. bulbous & acid & taciturn & un. avoid into
small pox. es & caves of desire. the drie ganaharra which
she had pho&phone the plumber about until she was like

blue in the face even tho it was such a long long way forum China & the S of France whe elvira & the mandarine-(s) really make tea in those black & gold coveteous lannscapes of glittering pic. tures of dragons on fire w/the v/ cardboard or celluloid canvas of mirage. jagg. ed plasket (s) of blue ice-collar around the black throats of volcanoes and the threes all clipp down & flim-cut to size in the valleys. so that even w/out closing her eyes he was like

walkin thru the walls of her mine w/his need/le & his lips now smilin & prissy & shaft . so she let him in quickly. she let him in quick. ly . like sweet. ly . swee. till. y . sleep. ill. y . slee. pilly w/only a likkle stick. illy sigh at the port as he enter the port. al. not day. not day. not dar ing to look out over her shoulder at her sleepering husbann the plumber who wd nvr now fish on the pink mourn
-ing slopes of -

Mount Fujiyama

the fountain
again while she gushin & geyser & geisha un-
lock by this locksmith this looksmith her lover

into this room w/ its map of green lake on the wall
w/ its stale oily draperies of no wind in the place
& the insects sleeping like tools
in the twilight of Trinidad or
Vir-

gin Gorda & a thin weep. ing wheel strung like
a fine
tune from the ceiling slow. ly tick. ing its time as it
turn

on the solitary life of the wire
& the motorbike of her dreams that had once barked
at her in the dark

rushg. in now at her roughly
& woof. in & woof. in as if it wd bite her. now asleep
in its tubes
& its grease

.

like her husband

'

so that she wd nvr again have to sweep
the dust & the dark & the husks of the dead
concrete slab of the room

like a good housewife shd

Mona 87 . **DS 94** . rev NYC feb & June 03. forom the postCallaloo see-true
seclusion
reformatt 22/23 July 03 & October 05 for New Directiones
w/a wonderful & blessèd unKpected palimpsest
NYC 7 Nov 05

xxxxxxxxxxxxxxxx My funny Valentine

for Nate Mackey

The night after my second eye

is re. move by the hang
-mans noose. me & my two one wife is in the miggle
of this room in like a whirlpool or serpent
of electric wires & she right font
catch-up in a loop as she cross the room
& she really already tangle

-up like in a lassoo unloose
around she fine St Valentine Day body
esp all up at de top rounn she breasts & shoulders
& i don't know how it get here/how she gett
like dis. and i askin her about
it as she try. in to come cross the room like to ford

me & stellin for help when this other
guy whose face i don't see
just as i don't see she face neither again after she get
-cross to where I like lying down in a deck or dock
or prostrate chair of the dream
and i can barely move to help her & try
as i try i cyaan ever rise

my hand so i cd hold on
to the top a the wall to help her while this guy like some kind
of a English. kind-a kind & concern & police like Jeremy I
-rons in most uh he flim
tho this isn't no Jeremy I
but real. like some-a dem broni livin off the flat

uh we ilann

an e like e comin towards me
to help she like
he inn see how she comin towards me she husbann tryin to get
up outta this chair of tirade

an he quiet & in. sistin & offerin
help/even tho she so close
to me now i can see the soft sea-weave
uh she skin & feel the half-halt heat that she breathe
-in &

watch
-in she turn how she turnin she black back to mwe
in this brown well-build uni. verse of mine
an be. ginnin to like let this guy help she out
-a she vi
-rus. while i have was to watch how he tellin she how to tek off
she blouse
a kind a soff off-white & flimsy sea
-islann stirrup in cool Trinidaddy crush
-cotton that she buy in-at CaveShepherd store
w/dese young rounn muttons all down it white front

- & sayin all this like quiet & tact
-full . showing proper respec
-(t) for his kind a cute immigration
- an i watchin these women a mine
from whe I am prostate

um. bottom she shirt like some meek scarifrice
of a blackbelly sheep of Barabados
she eyes down to the buttonholes
toggellin each one a dem wid she tum from de top
& the one-&-side sometimes slide a she finger
pushin them thru de hole wid she tum
& slidin & pressin dem down thu de hole like she playin
piano mbira

or onion

till all de gorgeous flash
on she back peel
-up & x
-plose from the dress
till she owl x

-pose to th view
in she black brassière wid-it black plastic hook at de back
& she plump & plum-colour skin all out
& facin this guy wid all she big rounn or
-ganics & powder all allmost all outta she bellows
& close close close to e face wid she power

so he had was to benn slightly down like frowards towards she
af
-front. bend

-in e knee to be closer & closer & like more careful & kisses
so he cd work like the lassoo awound she & up those brown
wonderful beasts - the slight shruggle of soldiers
& then care. full & slow
-ly up over
she grassbottle neck & the sweet wire hairs
of this once was my dearly belovèds
an she
keep. in she heads down not
sayin a word to this sword in my soul
an i watchin all a dis wheelin & turn-
in & tryin to get off de chair so i cd like stann-up & do what is
mwe shd be doin these wifes & Valentine morning

but a still weak weak weak in the tangle & trough a de dream
& she stannin up there a-
while where it happen a little a-
while after it happen
& lover. till she free from the wire that tingle & tripple
she foot

& the Jeremy-guy like e suddenly

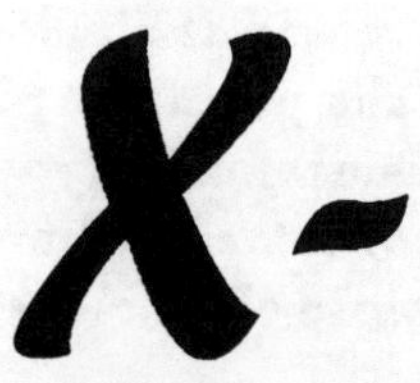

it & gone

and the brown daemon eyes of the once
was my di. was my die. was my di
-amond darling nvr once anymore like breaking towards

me
not ever she lookin towards
me

. she back to me back to me back
to me still in the black brassière of the room

lookin down at she breasts that she had was to daunce & x
-spouse to the wirll

& i remind/er re/minder before i wake up to wake up
how i make one lass chance to get up to get up . but try
as i try

mi cyaaan get de sun. rise up in mi head of balloon
so i cd grapple-on to dis top a de wall
. is so. is so. is so gnashlish & subtil & incontinent

New York rev Oct 99
forHambone 15 (2000) + Whispers from the cotton tree root: Caribbean fabulist fiction,
ed Nalo Hopkinson (2000); rev NYC June & July 2003 for NO . rev 25 26 Oct 05
NYC 7 Nov 05

ēĕā

'Dis road int got no Accompong'

4TH TRAVELLER

for
Dream Chad

About four weeks after Zea Mexican dead. three of us
was delivering canes in a cart into the depths of the bl-
ack country. Evvathing went well until we reach like
this village of the dead

At first. when we enter. we were happy to be there. as
we had been happy at each phase we reach at the end
of the long day's journey into night

We look around chattin at the late october ochre light
on the stone & wooden buildings w/their sense of brigh
(t) if not the fresh acquaintance of paint. *But whe were th
(e) villagers?*

No. body in the village square or under the halfway go-
lokwati tree. no one in front of their hovels . or howls .
no one shopping or anything like that. until our walkin-
(g). pushing the heavy heart of the canes. took us into>
this dark cul-de-sac of foreboding where this group was
sitting. dark caps pull down over dark fences w/a sense
of night of nothing happening altho they seem intent. ve
ry very intent. over the game they were playing - draug
hts domino whist - in the strange alien silence they wer-
(e) carr(y)ing

and they were making it clear. very very clear. even w/
out saying anything. that we were not welcome here -
that we cd not be welcome here - that this was not Zion
- that this was not the village that our burden sought . >
that Zion. *yes* (was this really the name(?)) was up a steep hill >
square squat abrupt gestures or what seem to be gestures even tho there was
no movement or change in their dark silhouettes underneath the vizard caps >
sweeping upwards to the heights up there out there somewhere >
in an even more directionless loom of the darkness. up
a steep tired hill. it wd seem. on the uttar side of the vill-
age and that it was *getting* late - almost too late - *why the foreboding?*
- & still nothing *said* - no word no real gesture under th-
eir gestures . shrug . dismissal . non-equivocal vocabula
ries of rejection. like crabs dis. playing dismal placards
squat & enclose w/in their crustacean boundaries of >>
petties pincers. clavés of silence

- *yes*

and we wd need help. especially at this hour. gettin la-
te. after the long honey sunlit journey into this night->>
blinding business

- *yes*

to get up there - directions & some. how money -

- *yes*

in pushing the cart up that last final disappoint-
ed hill outside this last village. since the road was bad

- *yes*

& wet & slippery & had like a very slow reverse curve -

they were very clear on this point. a quiet pleasure of glimmer from under
those down-playing eyes . or so it wd seem since there was really still nothing
from them x
-cept like this pressure of anger & rejection against us as from outer space

- like why were we there at all when we were not well/come when we had no
business there
when we had come wandering in so late in the sky towards evening
into their village

knocking against the door of the privacy of their secrecies
of - it suddenly seem - their quiet perhaps simple sorceries

for the game they were playing was maroon or m'ndin-
ka **warri/owarri**. i see it now. the board w/the round <
dug-out graves & the smooth horse-knicker seeds shin-
ing their bones in the smooth silence along their laps al-
ong the wooden table of the universe upon its wooden
trellis of deliberation

& our poor rejected labouring cart. slipping down back
the stark slippery slopes of the dark. the muscles in our
bellies hurting all along the shaft of the creaks. our kn-
ees bent & uncreeping farward

washed wasted breath

asperation of the dark

the donkey's four grey planted feet like thin veined stalks straining & like snapping. altho there was no wind and hardly even silence anymore on that hillside still far from the village of Zion that we had come so far to find to rest for the night in. according to plan. according to programme. & where we wd sell the day's load & so be able to begin again. fresh moorings. mornings

But we didn't even have time or the money for this. maroon (ed) out here in the tired shoes of discouragement & the >>> dust of fatigue while they play-out their jackass of low spades against us. dealing us out of their pact. placing us into **owarri** or worrying holes of lack or bad luck & fewture illusion. but we put a brave face of warri/or against them

like when a worn enamel tea-pot has fallen into the dirt into soft mud & its treasured tho ignored & thotless face is obscured for a moment

but you sink back down behind it in the dark world w/its so little water & bring it back up bring it back out & begin cleaning it face slowly slowly softly

w/the so little water. the palm of yr hand caressing its perhaps very ordinary features. the skin of yr hand against its brittle enamel. or perhaps there is a cloth which you plan gently against its urn crown ridd im carve making careful mathemagical gloves & oval (s) over & over again. finding & following the familiar domestic features of the tarn-ish(ed) but retrievable object

putting a brave face back upon it . despi-te all that mud & sullen animal hostility un der those old workingman khaki caps w/th eir dull once-shiney bus-conductor-like pe-aks pull down over their shadows w/out water of sunlight in this village of the da-mnn(ed)

So that we said - we were able to say to ourselves - since th-ey were not glistening - having not even spoken - no ton-gue in those blind heads no windows in those dark tonton eyes th at we still hadn't even seen. no ears in their blank walls of build-ings staring & unstaring at us as we had seen in the faces of yams or tumerous termites . in the soft untanned underground - that we wd go somewhe else. find somewhere else at this **wh ore** perhaps a warehouse or YMCA or a House of Corr ection or Charity - where we might leave what we had - the rest of our lord & whatever else might be owing - even tho it was clear that *there wd . be . no . return.* since we know that we wd be **attack** as soon as we turn away from tha (t) table of **warri**. leaving this village of the dead

tho nothing had still not been said & when even after
& against my instinct in this mortar
i had toll the foreman of that sitting goverment & judge-

matt - their heads still playing down un. sun un. sound >> un. smiling silence of the game in that *MIRG* village of the dead - which i discover later is GRIM spell backwords - whatever that may mwean -

'Goodbye' -

or perhaps even more ridiculous even more pusillanimous. it seem now - the crank of 'training' perhap (s). of being 'well-brought-up' perhaps to be nothing. to be thought. to be thought of. to be nothing . no. body -<

'Thanks' -

for what!
for silence? for hostility? for threats?

it was a sound inside my head like three. atts - dice shattering li ke gravel rain along the corrugated iron roof against our loaves < & not (yet) fishes

& yet i mutter something to be perhaps 'notice' - *that was it* - three. atts of dice against their utter noticelessnesses & utter noiselessness

as if we were not there . shd not be there

as if we were already like them . dead

and as i say. there come back no reply no notice. tho i know this silence mean a deadly planning . new ancient strategy of game . > lots cast against our louvres the future blotted out like their dark downcast eyes we nvr see w/out a voice

& for some daring desperation reason or un
-reason policy or ploy that bring surprise to me. light up my *yes*

while even
in the dream tho this was not a dream . this place . this
unplace where we are

(2)
i suck my teeth & dropp a small white stick-like
tooth-pick or perhaps some short-stick prick
of canetrash on the **warri** board
they were unseeing playing

& so we turn & left that group of silence
. that foreman & these all all-male sitters . bone
-yard squatters w/out sisters - Mercy Cornford Hope
- & we already lost the donkey & our cart
on that long up down
-ward uphill slide & slope where they had farmish us

(3)
My father have the torchlight & sometimes he move up
front & sometimes lagg behind since he was sick & you
cd see & feel how grey & broken down his brown skin<
had become & how e breathin hard & tryin not to cough

and w/that dry gravel soughing of like the water of ka-
unga crosssage

& even as i cost that stick of stone into that first village
that had made us turn our thoughts around & like go >
back go back go back. we hear a loud pierce ear out th-
ere w/in the darkness of the field we had not yet come
to come to come upon. but waitin out there for us like a
dark dark sheet of water or smooth slide of a stone slee-
(p)ing in our future

& i had thought it was my father's cry of pain & loneli-
ness despair & perhaps fear *<what! yr one father fear?>* but it was
nt him because the whole of us was still there stutterin
towards that sheer of future darkness & like our torch-
light had been lost or gone out after that one cry of the
match & we cd but try forget that he was sick while it <
was dark & we was walkin lonely poles of heads against
the sky which was like part of that dark plot of thank->
lessness against us. since they cd see & ambush us & we
cd feel our hair like moving stupid helpless head above
the leaf & heat our bodies mate . waiting the crack or
cutlass or however they had plan to cut us up or down
near that caul canefield of the village when we had hear
(d) ourselves say *quick*

>>and we was *quick*. ly down & entering this pain this canefield w/ its dark<<
mmurmuwater whisper of secrets & abysses that were close & birdless & take
away the breath our bodies make. crawling. fling flat down&quickly on our
bellies into a new farm of species. as it were. into the ancient coil&lash of the
serpent born before Adam. as old as the tree&the writhe of wind in the eden
& snake(d) vegetable green veridian eve. ening of clingers & maroons. like all
those who trie to escape into the feeling of swamp(s). out of the huts of their<
hearts. into the dreams of their chilldren. steel & unmannacle

and they was comin . like all mobs&masters. tirelessly beating the vegetation.
calling out to each other in the dark . lights flashing upon the sudden crabs of
red bauxite outcroppings. pathes tangle into crack. dark crash. cup. cusp. cl-
ump bosk. cockpit. yellowlovevine. jangle&jade of konnu. gully of breadfruit
kuku. the pale dwarf headless iguana coconut trees that we have become. call-
ing for dobru & mikey & walter & the light that fall out of our pocket(s) on>
the road & did we hear dogs barking. their hot heedless razor mouths & faith-
ful breath. . .we swimmming now on our bellies into this black mother world
away forom where we cd be seen against the flight of the sky. running galon-
(g) the horizon in the loud clear light of determination. of being perused & ab
use(d). even as we move like snakes now. thru the loud crystal stalks of shad-
owes which was like splashing shallow water around us running on the four >
hollow feet of our bellies. our eyes hot & lout & graven. each one for them->
self(s) under the canefield. . .

though still we hope that like dolphones there wd be some compass. some bli-
nd gravitational astrolabe of sound finding our way. stripped. stripped. flowin
(g) w/*macca* following a leader along the dark of our bellies. writhing away in-
to night. circling over&over in to the left/hand side of the god like when we >
pick up the teapot & polish it w/that kind of brave face & cotton raga before <
they begin burning the canes when they can't find us. bea. ing the bushes >>
bravura & dog-ear'd & eye. vile & the smoke all over the field before it is all <
over if it cd ever be ova. wallowing our green up chokin its water of sparks >
down our throats the heat crackling like stars & minnieroot. rats squealing >
out of their drip drowned desperate arasses. eyes trapp like our lost skills in >
there & nothing left to cry or crawl out of that drie(d)-out water with. after >
the fire & the look(ed)-for dawn

But it was still dark & the fire had not yet been lit

because we had **curved out on our bellies** out of that
locked invisible field of no bells no navigational lights far
from that village of the dead & the memory of our pursuers

tho they were still there . for as long as there was memory
there was still the possibility that it cd start up again
. scratch spark icicle

but we are out of the field & into the tradewinds again
. still blowing dark w/out respite . but on a bald patch
of hillside at the side of the wood of escarp
as if we had worn it out w/our

bellies

just the hard scratching grass & the little groundstones like
under the grass & like eucalyptus pungent & tart
in our nostril(s) instead of molasses & factory workings
& crack-liquor
& canejuice & lime & midnight-lights working the creak

& havock
of the mill & the thunder of water falling to cool the engines
of the night
& morning nvr coming up & when it come . rumour & red

but the herb-green respite grass held no terrors of great
mechanical swingers across the stars carrying the crushed
flesh of the hammock of fields on its robots >

this was like a brief beach or birth where we find ourselves
green again
& gentle & like beginning w/sweet
smell reviving our dreams

- if this was really possible after all that had happen
& not yet happen

for this canefield of womb or escape must have been
a great agreeable gushing tumour at the top of the hill
which we had reach from that village of the dead. tho there
was no Zion there neetha . at least not as we had x
-pected Zion

to be. and we had come out onto this gash & wound
in its side

& we are now slithering down this new other . this newly
altered slope
because as we lay on its side . we wd begin to un

-earth the sound of the dogs again & the plot against us a
-gain & the fear of those threshers try
-ing to destroy us so that we were unreasoning down
this slope now. still

hearing that hot crack-liquor of panic & slithering **down**
down down this happy side of the hill almost like when we
was chillren slidering **down into Brevitor's Cave**
& the marl slipping & we tryin to clutch at root & out
-crop & the helping hand of a tree-stump or angle or
avalanche of stone breaking the speed w/the heel feet
sliding ahead of us helpless like a trough or trench or urn
through the soft tumbling limestone & the loose stones
in their waterfall but further & further away

& we cd tell

like even in this dream. from that strange
village of the dead
& the sound of the beaters over our skills & the night
-blindness of the canefield w/its one offer of escape . like
sailing back on our bellies to the genesis of the world
. as the stones that are slippering w/us became like more
& more form
-al as we slowed towards what seem to be the bottom
of the hill
or hull & there were **steps** of stone now turn
-ing ruins
as if we had. as chilldren. **found some old reservoir**
where the island stored its valour
tho these stone steps seem larger. somehow. & older
& like more ruin

& i am jump
-ing down them fast fast fast
still under this steeple & angle of de
-scent. still w/in this humming rim
& memory of revolt & the danger still there because there
was as yet no end no village of rest or horizon

and i was wondering where the others now were
tho i cd hear like one other behind me. or near me. clearly
un. clearly. tho i did not know who it was tho it was not
my father. someone younger & the other two
of us were perhaps still out there on the hillside

or - i tried not to think
of it - no memory no imagination - **wd this make it not happen?**
- not have happen?

- that there is one other back there in the canefield
of escape. burnt
or drown in its waters - but perhaps not. since there is al
-ways hope
in this dream. ever since i had throw(n) that stick of stone
against the foreman's **warri** board. and the tree of us
was runnin thru these huge rooms
of rum of the ruin factory. thru subtle subterranean sound
the walls high & bleak & mottle. the ceilings high
& unseen. the water splash/ing somewhe memory . the echo
of footsteps running running running
- multiplication of clip/clops tho there was no hoof no heel
because there were no shoes or i. ron down here bolted
& running & the grey tuning to like gam

-beige as we reach the stagnant statement of water
covering the floor at the bottom of the stairs

for this was more than a ruin factory of stain
tho not yet palace
as i had seem in films of dreams . but a GreatHouse

yes

immemorial plantation underground. chambers. bedromes
balloons of sound. hi-fi-like rats' ratchets clambering up
the walls of the dungeon

& we jumping over holes & wells & water carpets
of fungus . green steaming lignumvitae
shadows of perhaps stalactite & stalagmite chalking

of bones. but glimpse(d) like only one long cool silver
silence from the corners of my ghosts
eyes echo/ing hollowgloom & the steps steep step down

& sometimes slippery w/moss & neglect & the years & years
of the cyclops of ungreatness ruined & leading no
-where

so we decided to at last stop. out of breath
w/that rise & fall/ing of the chest which meant not
desperation now but a ceritain fee. line eagle of well
-being health

of having *come through* a doorway
of success & a curtian soft sweating of safety of keys
as if we knew that there was no longer any Midas here
who wd call out the dogs & the profits of doom
& try to hout us all off. choosing tho a good careful spot
to enjoy safety in

i keepin to the straight & arrow of our flight. my friend
the 4th traveller
whoever it is. now w/me. going up a flight of stars

at an angle to whe we was running where there was like
a dark jutt or aardvark slant where she too wd feel safely

- *so is it a 'she'?*

but there was no sound of others no sun or cloud or sol
-ace of my father
or of pursuing voices splashing light after us in this new
underground of the world . this underhouse of the dead
as it were

and becoming more & more so as we stood there listening
to its nothing & its
stale stagnant memoirs & its water dripping & staring
down the walls
of the ark & its long green carpets of silence so far away
from the hillside now & the canefeel of serpents long
perhaps passed away but still out there burning on fire

(5)

and in the dark village of memory w/its dead playing <<
cards - domino or whist romee or suck-de-well-dry-dry
& Mexican dying in the absence of my father who was
certainly not now in the cave w/me w/us & how i had <
seem so cool as they say as she lay dying there in her <<
bronze fever skin not at all like my father who had lost
our torchlight when it was darkest. our heads xpose to
the dark of the w/hole village of indifference

& it was like i was bending down scooping water into <
the cup of my hand cooling my face watching her dying
so that as i say i appeared cool - *how else?* - who or how els-
(e) - *cd i be?* - twisted & destroyed in that canefield on the
edge of this village of the dead

and i had bought two television set. xtravagance of des-
peration. escape into minefield of unmemory anemone <
setting them burning & playing till morning when the <
sun come up on their bleak eyeless gazers. the stations
all gone home to sleep since soon after midnight since <
this wasnt no holiday & only the planets & stares & like
white static of moonscape moving over their faces & i
proppin upon my elbow of sorrow watching the animal
flowers of her eyes of when she cd walk talk laugh like

a silver bell flashing & they was callin me hypocard be-
cause i had bought these electronical 'things' when i sh
(d) have been worrying & because they thought i was >
watchin the sereens when i was looking at her picture <
& not being able to hear how the light had narrowed to
a ffine bright thorn or strobe or diamond. so that the fic
tion flickering flickering flickering from those faces was
like as i say a scoop of cool water w/which i wash her fa
ce

but they use some good ole Jamaican
white rum of proverbs against mwe. about deceivers &
hypocrites like how *craven choke puppy* & how *scarnful* >>
daag eat dutty puddin whatever dem might mwean

but because they was proverbs & dancefall parables ab-
out *pussy* & *pusey* & *sawlfish* they was *believe* like gospel <
all along the rim of the villages of Byall & Warsopp to
defeat me

for when she die. it was me who had *cry out* that night >
outside the village of the damned w/my father & the oth
ers. one of who was waitin w/me now in this city of un-
natural marble ruins underneath the burning canefield-
(s)' cinders by the headless coconut trees w/the cart &
the load of canes for the village of Zion which we had >
not yet reach which we might not now nvr reach & me

left here on the floor w/the empty ricegrains television <
face of morning looking at her face. looking for her eyes
which they say had not yet died & were so dark so very
dark& tenochtitlán like her lashes full of morning in the
morning & travelling down the sky of time & changelin
(g) light & *quetzl* to evening & tonight even tho she was
only sleeping w/sometimes her hand touch. ing her chee
(k) of the angels as if remembering something like some
thing she said she wd tell me but didn't - *yu kno how it go* -
deep & scoff & flowing like confetti

like only now she dead & seem to be sleeping . which is
why they say that she wasnt dead . even tho i kno now<
that she is she is & i touch her arm almost like i soffly<<
pinch her as i wd have done if she was sleepin as i have
alway(s) done when she sleepin just a soft quick tick of
her flesh like that. no rip or tear or trip into time whe <
she seem to be so war\so war\so warm\so time. less\ & <
so difference from the television scream - *warm too but so so*
differently timeless - w/the sky in it face as in hers and the <
morn. ing breaking into leaves into tears into soft heave
(s) of showers i suppose into last kisses into like shak-sh
ak shake softly into water into the sound of a rainy day

and in the middle of all this i
cd see the visitors. led by a >
tall bespectacle deconstruct-
ionist critic. his smirk. the sm
ock of his body coming to mo
ck me. his head held high. all
his eyes shock bright. look- >
in out like his followers foll-
owin on little sticks or lanth-
orns of language like crabs >>
or scarabs on poles advancin
behine they self-proclaim & >
scurryin leader. wav. in they
puffy pink pin. cers like box-
ers or boers. like the villager
(s) plyin they romee or whist
outside the rumshop(s) but >>
lookin out new almost x-tinct
but alert & X. pectant . X.pec
tin to see me like a clock or>
cock or cork leakin heartbeat
towards when & where they>
wd knock knock knock at my
door when they wd ring whe-
(n) they wd strike

 .

pectin to see me perhaps any minute or second coming >
out of the house of the water of grief to- *yes*- greet th-
em. to at least meet them but i - *<hypocrite lecture>* - cdn't
i cdn't not then not that day not at that time of alarm
even if it mean that they wd offer me their false fruit
& mead of the bad food of reviews & see to it that i >>
wasnt publish or fêted again

but i dock down tuckin my head down into my belly clo-
sing my eyes like *asterisks or tasks* so that they wd >
not be able to see the risk of my stars in the green sha
dow of glass in the mirror of the dead tv set & i went >
out onto the middlepassage of the hillslide w/the other
(s) & the donkey-load of canefields on our head(s) en->
route to the village of Zion which as yu know we nvr >
reach tho three of us went back out & up back up that
slippering hill. side of spirits where we find our father
hurt & wounded yes & slow but clambering down the >>
sleep hillside & we carrie him the next day on to the >>
nxt village further along the ridge of despair where th-

ey were having like Carnaval . drums flags fifes men in
masks crocus-bags-jumpin-&-trump-in-&-tumpin-goombay
&-tukkin-wid-ruk-a-tuk-boom-box-&-cymbell-&-flute so-
me kind-a celeberation of yam & harmattan . so that all
the lights were on & bright & they was like blue & sun-
light & chilldrens choppin out macca & grass from rounn
the soff edges of the pond & they was sayin in the vill-
age square. in front of their houses & horomes. as it we
re. whe they went to buy& eat sardine & biscuit & pig-
tail or pone. or juss sittin here out in the sky of their <
talk

and they was sayin that the 4th Traveller had not survi
ve . tho how s/he die(d) they did not know or perhaps
they did not care or dare to find out or say anything >>
perishing alone out there on the night of the hillside in
side that in. visible canefield. not of her dreams but >>>
our noiseless galloping nightmare nr this dark village of
the dead where i now sit in this yard as the foreman. >
digging yr graves in the game of yr luck or yr warri. >>
dealin my cards in the insolence

created Kingston May 1988 . first publish *Callaloo* XII:1(1989) w/ several revisions since . inc Kingston June-August 1993 & NYC June 2003 . esp June 15 & 16 when i begin to find out a little more about the 4th Traveller. reform for NewDirections 23-24-25 July 03 (all-night to 5:35am & there's quiet sunlight outside!) when because of loss of Sycorax memory. certain dying fonts. like Salt Eliot's poems they are. will not stay will not stay in place will not stay still now early june 04 04 04 04 and almost impossible all NYC night 21 October 2005 & well into the morning of the 22nd

NYC night 21/22 October 2005

NYC 7 Nov 05

DREAM HAITI

an antiseptic critic of inglann or angloAmerica who
love Derek Walcott & why not
& the flowingly restrain poems of Ian McDonald
on the great Essequibo River of Guyanas

- says of my work -

poor lute. poor flute. poor ragged five stringed fingers of my star guitar
- that mwine celebrate -
sad thing - apparently bad thing - what im call

'the [un]seemingly endless

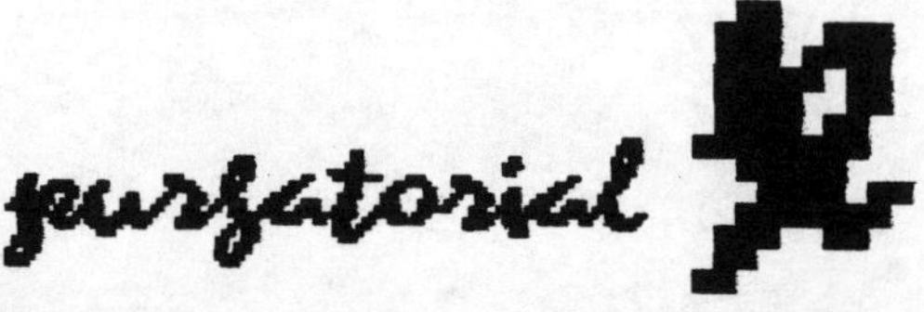

.perienz of black people'

for

David Rudder

Haiti I'm sorry
We misunderstood you
One day we turn our head
And look inside you

Haiti I'm sorry
Haiti I'm sorry
One day we turn our head
And restore your glory

. Joan Dayan . Murat Brierre . Edwidge Danticat .
The Boukman Eksperyans

◆

Alex Haley
himself 20 yrs in the US Coast Guard who die today 18 May 92 age 70
while this is born

◆

the many more thousands gone

The sea was slake grey of what was left

of my body . and the white waves
I memember

they was like v/snake on my skin
& they keep comin in at this soft swishin diagonal diamond

the blow & wet metal sides of my nerve
where the US Naval Coast Guard cutter was patrollin
all along the borders of the Mexicans & my brothers –
in what was call in the dream . the Time of the

//// mi write

Shanté Chacmoul

. ask WHAT NAME BAHAMAS GIVE HAITIES WHO COME ADOBE

BEG WOROK ////

And it was not that we was goin anywhere if you see
what i mean
–
i mean we was not goin anywhere altho the ship
was movin
i suppose & the sea was also movin impeccable
& so was the waves
& yet in my dream it was juss like on board
anyship anytime anytide
–
& they was that up/thin & thick/down movemant &
soft ooze of things creakin & tryin to fall
or actually fall–
in/off even tho evvating on board that hill–
slide was suppose to be slip–
shape if you know what i mean about Bristol fashion

& something like bells on the horizon either still
like a sword & shine like an affordable razor-
blade of light . or goin up & down slowly & softly grey
like the ship in my head w/the nerves breakin out
sibilant & white like a long line of voice rollin softly

›

the sigh of the ship & our feet clangin restless/ly up &
down the studded metal stairs of the sough
muted agony w/that strange smell of something like
hidden linseed oil & closed-in space & the mem-
ory of cabins of mal-de-mac & wantin to throw

& havin to run compulsively somewhere
to scuttle it down the hatch

& where there was like nothin we cd do about anything
now that we was there in the dream of the ship
waitin as I say for these

[illegible]

in a strange land

I do not know why i am here – how i come to be on board
this ship – this navel of my ark –
w/my nerves as I say comin & goin & my head spinn-
in soff-
ly & beginnin to wet & giddy & my heart pushin hard ❯
the daylight of my body & swishin for the peace
& darkness & the spice of gumbo Sundaes
since i am suppose to be a poet not a coast guard cut-
ter or fireman or one or two others on this deck
standin by the ribs of the railins whe they was these
hard white life-savers or

that you pulley over yr head like tyres or

of survival

& you swimmin there in the dark or the water
& throwin them scream-
in to some-
body else out there w/a splash-up face & a hann
like the flash
of a fish or the feather of a sunlit bird tryin to dream
or drown
& they was suppose to be some kind of rope or chord
of music or a anthology call

that iere had senn w/her love from the i-
lann of flamingoes

that you gripp in yr hann when you toss it white little
sweetie over the side w/the legend

US
COAST
GUARD
GUTTER

stencill & chill upon it both side in black
on wjat
i suppose is suppose to be like top & bottom

US
COAST GUARD
GUTTER

& then

RETTUG DRAUG
TSAOC
SU

w/i suppose the

US COAST GUARD
GUTTER

part for yr head & the

RETTUG
DRAUG TSAOC SU

for yr foot or coffin

—

tho of course it was round & not at all
like yr foot or coffin

or the coffle
of yr memory that you might one day have to jump thru
on one of those blue or yellow or scarlet airlines w/the

HOSTESS

stannin up in front of you & evvabody else xcept the crew
wavin she limbs about & smilin like the palmfronds
& hardthighs of some lonely or crowded beach & pretendin
to be doin all these things w/yellow & whistles & no pain
or snarl since we are not
in the air & my head is like gettin giddier & giddier as I try
to write this w/the blinds down against the light
& my nerves so tight that i'm kinda bline stannin up in front
of evvabody & not bein able to see

SALKEY

or Sundee or the Port-au-Prince of my youth
anymore

& i often wondered what it wd be like out there far
away from my homeland on the flat
Atlantic w/io & i only head above the thatch
roofs of the waves & my hands lonely like creation up
& down the rub-a-dub & knub of the white ahab stump
of my elbow & my no feet under the white whale of water
since no/body cd see them in that kind of only gaol
& sickness of the sea & its thicknesse anyway

&

as i say not one a we know what we was doin there
when we shd have been somewhere else writhin poetry
or whatever & i notice in the dream how carefully no one
didnt know where they was either/which after all is not
supprisin since we had all been at sea for a long time
long time now - evva since i had pack my suitcase before

PETIT MATIN

high up above Morne D'Estagnes
in all that mist of Kenscoff & bamboo & Filao & did not even
have time to scrape the ashes from the fireplace
before I was down the hill bound for those

tuilleries behind the Iron Market

whe we was to meet the man w/the canot

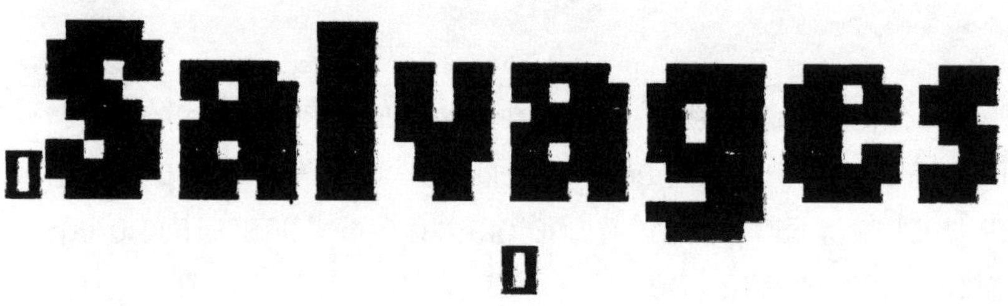

& i remember coughin & thinkin

SEA COME NO FATHER

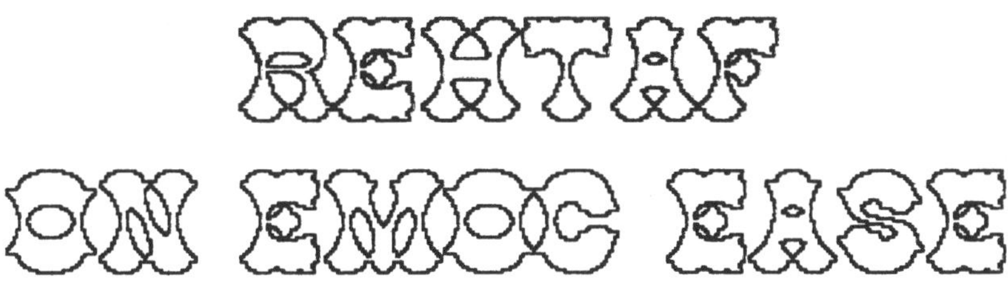

as if i was already turnin the leaves of the waves for a long long history of time before i cd get back to sleep & in anycase nobody had written anything serious since Mexican die & the Gilbattery of 1988
i think it was because of what was bein said of

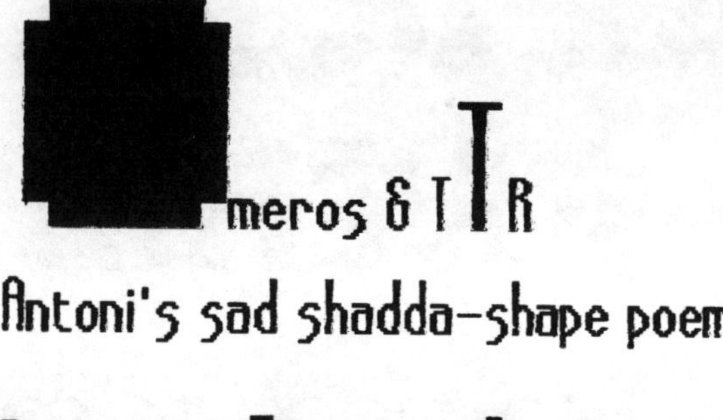

Divina Pastora

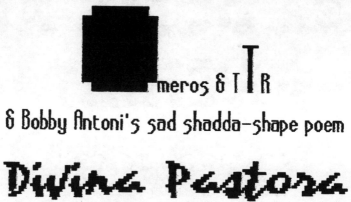

S.

we was all standin they in that kind of windy silence
of this dream – not close together
ofcourse since we was all artists & strangers to each
other & not soldiers or sailors or dwarfs as i have to
go on insistin
even tho we was all on the same trip as

had seh so many years ago
& all on the same ship & the same slopin deck
& there was no doubt about that since there was rapes
neatly toiled & there was the smell of cool & salt & gun-
metal oil & the first thing that shd have warn
– us that something unusual was happen-
in outside of whatever we shd have been writin was when

Sun

Bryan

appear on the water like a kind of livin **life** buoy

but it was only his face there in the shape of a smile
or what look like a smilin triangle made out of tinnin
as if he was the work of

Murat
or Grègoire or Marèshal

or a sheet of soff metal or a lief of cardboard more
pobably – painted or treated to look like tinnin or metal
or the wrok of

taruM
or eriogérG or laĥséraM

only – as you see – somewhat backwrods

& he pass quite closed but swiftly by like a kind of
sea-island kite

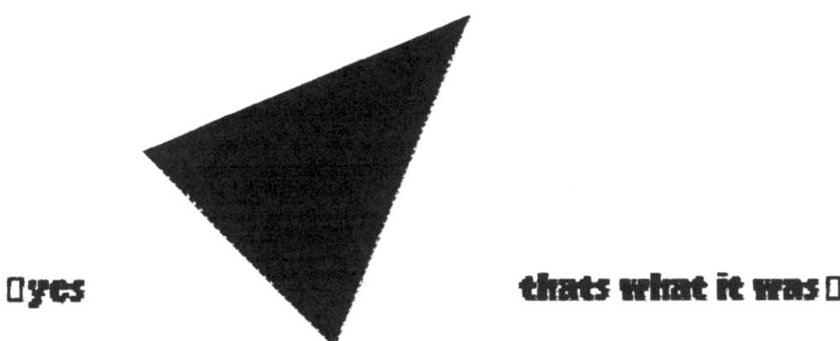

on what the pilot or captain or somebody w/a microphone
pobably on the bridge or up in the sky
of the rigging – tho we hardly ever look up there
because of the stars – since evvating was like moving

so strangely
& if & when we did

we wd like find ourselves falling hard on the dirk
or not being able to pay our homage or balance our bills
& pitchin forward or sideways towards the railins
& the frontiers of our nation which was all
we had between ourselves & the high nervous condition
of the impeccable surge & breathe of the seas out there
& the captain was saying

that the Sun Bryan object

- which is how you wd have i suppose to describe it -

was on a

□starboard course□

- whatever that mean -

rockin from side to side like a cock or a pen-
dulum. as if he was sus-
pended from the top of his pointed head
above the coumbite of water
while the base of his face which somehow -

-
now that i think back about it & have been able to revise & correct what i got up to write down far too hurriedly early this mornin as we went on board the canot
-

& i remember feelin v/v/cold even tho we was

in that boat designed as the TV commentator
kept shayin/like to cry or carry only

13 or **14** or **15**

& this kite & rockin triangle of him seem to contain
all the old rest of his body/i mean like his mouth w/his font
teeth missin as usual & his chin & his shoulders & his shirt
& chest all down to his belt & waistbuckle & the torn dirty
trousers of the donkey farmer

□ **when he choose to be a farmer that is** □

& his feet like tuck up & folded under evvating just like us

on

the tief of his face a deceptive assassin of light
tho as i say you cdnt see that & indeed you cdnt see nothin
but this rockin & smilin triangle of the head rollin swiftly
pass the

Coast Guard Gutter

& like tic/tockin tic/tockin from side to side from the top
of the clock of his hair
& we all lock at each other because we had heard that

MADAME

MARGARET
EUGENIA
AZUCHAR
MARKETPLACE

had at last gone up w/her harsp gruff whip & chauffeur of a voice to IT or perhaps it was Penlyne to see what was goin on & to give some kind of support &

macoute

to the farmers in response i suppose to my tele/phone call years before to her on that bleach of shells where she had been able to pick up a large pink

lambi

or conch in she hann w/out bein cut by the sharp heard cuttin edge of the

as had happen to me when i was a likkle bwoy on a Bank Holi-day when i was too young really to remember anything else xcept the dunes & the bright light on all that sand of the no hair of my youth & dazzle & the red blood from my finger oomin down into all the coral beaches i wd ever stand on sin ce & lookin at birds & fishes far out on the horizon

& by the time i got up there evva/one was of course stalkin
about the visit & how flate it was of her to come even tho it
was clearly too late to overstann anything about

it

& evvating was like growin bark green again
over all the morasse & the chasm & the awesome lann-
scrape that had covered the golden flutes of the bamboo
that she had never seen clumped

so that she cd smile in the sunlight & feel it warming
her pain & the underside leafs of her face & her dark
lizard glasses & opening every cribbit & corner of her skin &
pouring like waves all round her into rocks & eddies &
responding to the colour of the daylight & the chlorophyll

so that she was able to come to a firm political decision
pretty soon after that – about 'commanding the heights
of the economy' & 'levvel playingfields
of 'light at the end of the tunnel'

etc etc etc

& departed all the villagers of our shorne hill-
side to the deck of the ship where we was now passin Sun
Bryan & looking out for Mexican &

The Haitian Refugees

tho nothin had happen as i have been tellin
you for what sheem like a long long time & we had started
to relax under the tall grey pool of the ship when someone
shouted the way

Sancho Panzo

must have shouted for

COLOMBE

12 October 1992

& we all run to the railings again since it wasnt rainin or anything like that – grippin them tightly of course since we didnt wish to fall into what the sailors call drink & in any ease we was all afraid of doin so all the time just as i notice that when i went up to Penlyne or try to cr-
oss any bridge of dirt or psyche of stone at

or slipp down the slopes of coffee & pimento to one of

Neville Dawes

v/early Jamaica morning poems

that i was like afeard of heights even tho
it was a landscape of sounds & sweet ears that give delight
& hurt not –

which we now know it wasnt –

so that i fe/fe/feared i felt

□ it felt something like that □

that i wd fall & tumble down into the valley or rather into the dark green grievin hole of laplasse far far below/ which was like the end of the story i am writin of my life or all my life/i cant remember which – but i notice that the railings or stations & stanchions or whatever they was naughtically call – was like mode of the same material or metal as our fingers & the palms of our hands

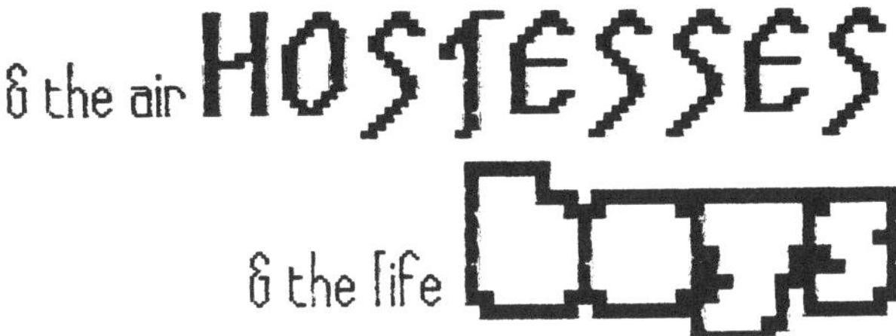
& the air HOSTESSES
& the life boys

suddenly out there in the hard water like flyinflish
or mullets or whales or poipoises or like

land ahoy

like

Guanahani

or a rainbow out to sea

or

anything starlin & unusual that people on board the

MiddlePassages

rush to see to relive the ruins of what becomes like limb
or limbo on board the bells of the ship

& each one had like a white head that flash back & forth to a black head just floatin by in the water & each one of them had like this great wide open mouth cryin out for they country & callin to us across the narrow valley of their children to help them or come fish them out or unhook them as if they was congoreels or lobster or negatives w/thin wet tentricles which of course they was or had become tho we didnt know then that the

Salvages

had try climbing up one more griji or hill
of crumbling gl ass just out of sight of Pt
Sérene even before we had gone like stumblin
down into that dark blue siege & surge
the bar/bar/ bark & barrack/the dogfish
dogdark barbwir [e] of these shark
water/gates like into the poisson & prison &
dungeons of guinée & gorée &
the fort-de-joux & the plâce-des-armes
at gonaïves & défilée &
dessalines dessalines dessalines
& the blk pickets at

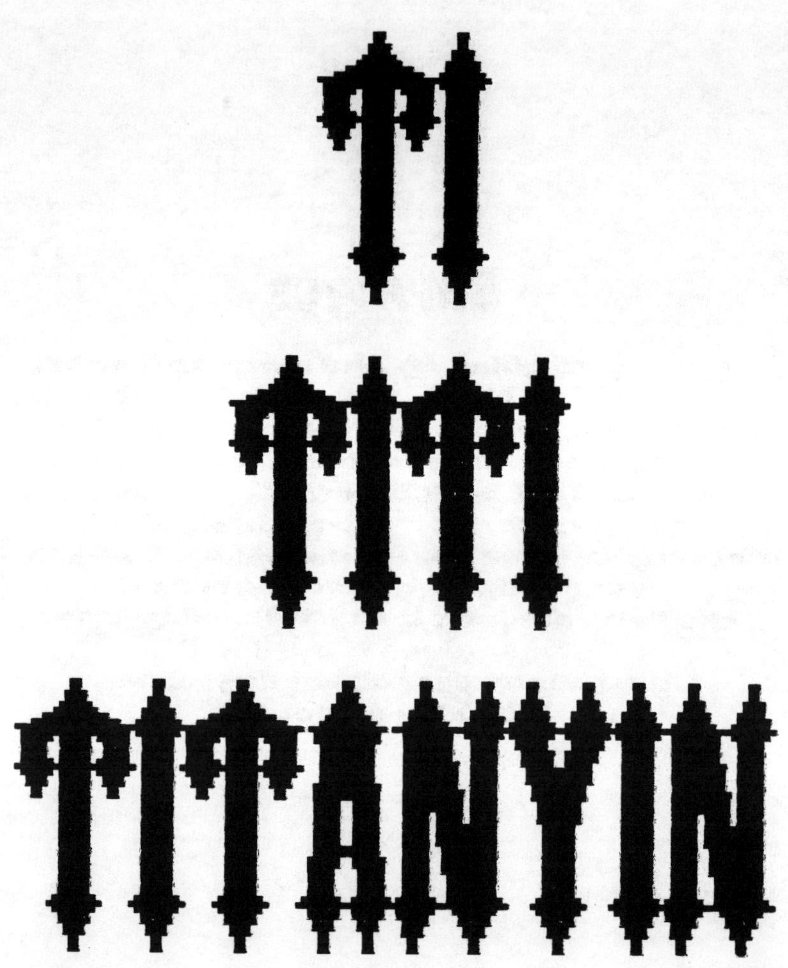
TI
TITI
TITANYIN

that ancient sound of the water churling into our lives like these hard hard leaves that dont allow us to breathe or even dream ourselves out of its convent of mirrors

that went down into like somebody blind & convicted &
i remember that it was like some dark gaoler of convex of glass was like lockin us up against// & against// & i cd hear the long echo/ing noise of the metal doors of my lungs clanging shut in our

face as if it was Christophe on La Ferrière walking that sloe corridor of water

as if it was Toussaint Legba all the way out on Napoleons joyless eyeless island of torture on the glacial seas of the Jura

& we were trying to reach the lifelines that were made of the same material as the thongs of our fingers & the webs of our skin altho we cd hardly see that nobody had started throwin any of them overboard to help us

déchouke déchouke déchoukaj

& there was so much goin on all above & around us
what w/ the ferrymen shoutin & fightin for survivors tho we was all quite dead &
bloated by this time

& some of us had even start floatin on our blacks up to the scarface which is when i suppose we cd barley see that nobody wasnt throwin no lifelines nor booies nor anything like that towards us & in anycase i didnt have time to think any of this down even if i cd have . in all that crushin & cryin & fallin into these crashin

&

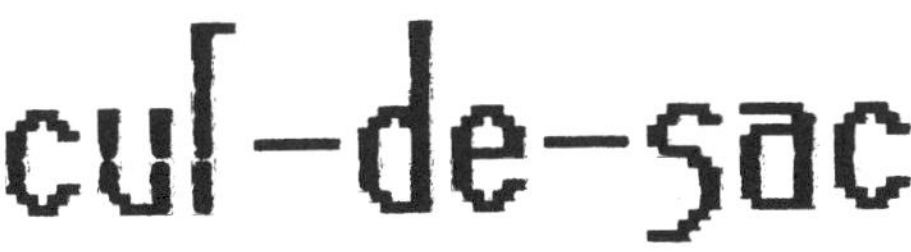

heights that i always fear like a grave & love like a govi
& i know that they was tryin to tell us
w/their black eyes filled w/splinters & marassas of water & pipirit pipirit pipirit
& the whole wide world of the thunder of

Atacama

blowin so *bleakly* into our faces that they couldnt see far less
see us anymore

and when I look up again from this crowded boat of
my brothers & the single star of my sister

- the **US Coast Guard** cutter
scowling above us -

the skull in front of me capsizes

- screams calls cries -

the green tide ruining us all the way back to distant
Dakar

to the dungeons of the cyclops'
Gorée Gorée Gorée Gorée Gorée

the salt in the eyes of my rainbows. my hope fading
faster than my heartbeat. the water like silkworms
now in the chunnels of my mind in the cracked
ghastly tunnels of my wrongs

there is a huge globe around me like the moom
there is a dead sun breathing some-
where in the cracked glass of this endless morning

& I see this drift . this greem . this coconut
maroon perhaps from Goave from Gonaïves
the little black head bobbing on the water

& i lean over the sleep side of our boat. titled already into all these depths into all these passing deaths. these *-yes-*

'endless

purgatorial

passages'

- **if you can call it that** -

this swift catch from the sea in my hand
held up like a dolphin or lantern or like papa agoue
weeping weeping weeping from the fresh salt tears
of the sea -

this bwoy. this likkle bwoy. in my hand
like a dolphin but dead . drown(ed) -

you have seen him on tv before

juss this glimpse juss this shot dripping w/history - clear out of the water *for all our bowls to see* - his hands folded politely before him. his soft sea body hanging heavy. swinging lightly quietly from like the old clotheshanger hunger of my hand. the gree (n) shirt that his dripping mother dress him in. his eyes close. his mouth as if it never know drowning - *as if he wd open his eyes. out here on Bahama wa-ter. as if he wd smile. as if the Atlantic wd shine fr-om his mouth like the new morning he dream of his father the carpenter his mother the owl*

and all the world waits the world watches as i drop him back
down w/the splash

- let me say it -

that e nvr deserve

back into the water
that e nvr deserve that e nvr nvr nvr
deserve

that e nvr deserve

& yu chide me fe
chantin like
this? fe lament
=ing this seem
=ing perpetu
=al pogrom & pro
=gram like this?
this
season on
season persist

=uant anomie?
for tryin to ghost
words to
holla
this tale?

1234567890

that he will swim back to Africa now he is drown .
that the shadow of this

Coast Guard
Cutter

of blockade
has nothing to do w/his coconut head & the cost of
his arms folded sleeping in salt?

that we are they broders & fellow writers bound to them by all
kinds of travellers cheques & the content of our character as if
we didnt memember how they have put on they shoes that

afternoon - bending down

to their blue washicong pumps to tie the black laces before
takin us up to Jacmel to Marigot
to Pétionville to scroll thru the markets of Limbé & Limónade &
Labasse & Petit-Goave to see wher

Hector

Hyppolyte live

tho of course they say nothin at all but
jus went lobbyin lobbyin by w/their
heads up & down in the corr□e of
water & they arms still vainly
tryinto reach Miami & Judge
Clarence Thomas & the US Supreme
Coast & their mouths wise open wise
open & ounsi
drinkin salt & dream & the gold-
en sound of the court like

LA CR TE-
A- PIERROT

&

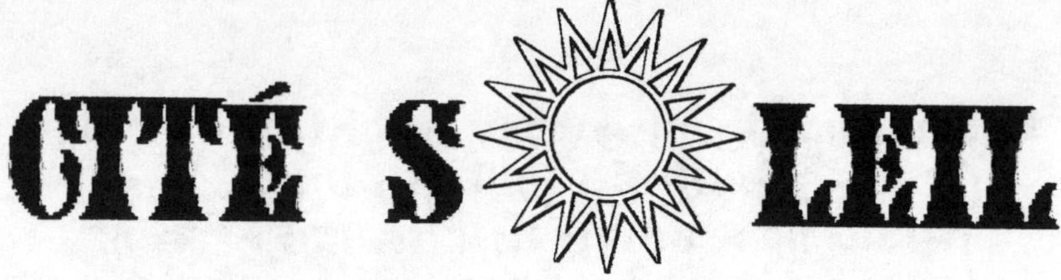

'and I hear the weight of the river/of the ocean all the time. It creaks beneath my voices like a wooden platform under a tonton/of water/thunder of mountain hideous rock. It opens up to swallow all who step in it – man woman monfi mafi tout timou. as if they bellies are weighing w/aba w/sto

nes down down down down'

while we stann on the soff hard deck of the

Coast Guard

Impeccable

watchin them poem

OS (1994). Cow
Pastor March 2000 version w/slight & then more voiolent enjambent adjustments NYC June + July
2003 w/last page adjust NYC 23 Oct 05

SALVAGE (S)

throughout New Spain there is a kind of snake which is the length of a pike and as thick as the arm; the head is as large as a hen's egg on which they have two plumes; at the end of the tail they have a rattle which makes a noise as they glide along. They are very dangerous with their teeth and with their tail; nevertheless the Indians eat them after having taken away the two extremities

>placard □Brown University Library, Providence, Rhode Islann<

The dreamon

has become so real
that I wake Chad up to ask her if she had seen
it - as if it had either really or already happen
or had we been watching it together on TV before she
fall asleep in the sea of our bed And there was this deep
dull soft sensation in my cock as if some
-body was trying to wrench or pull it
out or off or something like that

. it begins w/ this friend of mine on the high seas <

perhaps on the dark heaving blue brocade
around our island. riding this open boat like a horse
over the soft ruins. A laughing happy guy
. like one of the Bebe's on Browns Beach
or a descendAnt cousin
of one of the spider- or lightermen from an earlier story
or a young fisherman or son of some fisherman
or crabber from Dundlo or Lightfoot Lane or Bayland
up behind St Paul's Parish Church whe my Godma
Joe use to live <

or just a guy who had this boat that he own
or had borrow
-(ed) or had use of or was looking-after for somebody
or whatever. And this day or sometimes we use to be
out in it w/him. sittin & laughin
on the wooden cross-boards - or *thwarts*
- and holding onto the border or gunwale when the
boat hit a wave & bangg up into the water & spray
& sky juice

air w/ that woof after the bang along the hull & then
come back down w/ more like a shudder & thudd
and as I say. we were all laughin
& happy & half-naked & ball-headed & hair

-less w/ the sun
hot where the water & spray quickly dried out on our
skin into a salt spot or smear on the ponds of our
chest(s) or our thighs
& it was like copper or rather like bronze
all over against the blue
& the grey & the green & all that move
-ment & agitation & landlessness since we were some
miles out beyond the sigh

of our island And I never know that he/who sometimes
seem to be me sometimes even me. was in anyway ill

or feeling ill or having problems of any kind
or anything like that. that in other words

he was like me. w/ nothing wrong that I am aware
of - quite the opposite in fac

there was so much happiness & energy & future &
sense of bias
if I may use Wordswroth's words & well-being which
we had learn in school <

our bellies flat. bodies flit. muscles ready to go
anywhere & do whatever we like like swimm
-ing or jumping overboard & holding our underwater
breaths forever & diving down down down down
the cool crystal bondage till our ears hurt

or floating on our back untale the sun went black & it
seems we were about to fall asleep or drift
off to St Vincent or see sharks & holes
& we felt that if our boat ever sink
we cd swim all the way back to Holetown or Black
Rock or wherever one of our rivers wash its freshwater
face in the sea <

tho sometimes there was this sensation behind my eyes
like a kind of hand/clap or mist & a slow

soft steady pyrexia in the bones of my hands
which recently a nurse
who took them both in her prayers one good
night after a poetry reading. to thank. I think. or
congratulate me & was surprise. she said. how hot
the fronds of my palms were. as if my whole friend
& body was an ember or rather a tree I cd barely
remember. that had been set secretly alight in the
woods & the flame had like crawled inside from the
roots like into the tall ariel trunk & was hiding & eating
the lubes & circuits

inside so that the tree was **be hold**

too hot
& golden & smouldering out there in the forest

but no one know that it was on fire & wd nvr know
until the like reed crimson golden water of sparks
break out into its face & its leaves & the sweat
of its branches

until it was like the whole sweet canvass city of art
& cathedrals & falling jewelled arches was on fire
in that forest - which came unto me un

-awares like a kind of alien or stranger or what in
another lifetime later they wd call '9/11'
that like had everything in its nothing to do w/me
whatsoever. that I cdn't x
-plain or talk bout as if it was happening underwater

all this ice & pyre

-ia & refraction in one dream
& worse. that I cd do nothing about. it seem
tho it was only there sometimes & to tell you
the truth I hardly pay it no mind until after it was over

tho as I say the nurse that evening had like *reach*
it & *touch* it & *divine* that. beyond my control my

metabolicrate

- (that was the ţerm she nuse) - was too high too swift too swimming away
from me/ w/ me like some kind of Mona Passage
or Gulf ScreamDrift tugging warm or cold at our bellies >

but I had laugh it off tho what she had said so sadly. in her way
(though she was smiling too/at my laughin it off) must have worrie me onto
the open boat or broad-belly motor barge riding waves out on
the streaming high seas or dreams in the harbour

but there was **no problem**

until the day we met. out on the high sierras
these *guarda-costas* or as it turn out. sea-doctors or pharmacists
or something like that - some serious or at least serious
-looking white guys like from the CIA one of who seem to be like
my ole frenn Randy Burkenheit form

Dream had

& even **Valentine** & Haavaad >
& there were a few others. dress I think. in white nasal
uniforms & short pants as if they had come off a corvette

or crusade or navel
LOVEBOAT

& there was in this white sleek or sloop
that come up

alongside our lighter one morning as if they was

sleeping for fish - w/all they wares & wir
-es & radar & flags flying & flashing &

POWER

& all kind-a techno*logical* contradictions - for lobster
& skeet & catfish & tropical algae & sponges & snorkel
& plankton & sea-wasps & sea-plate & sea-roaches - or
pertending to. do. so. as it turns out >

or rather doing so while really conducting whatever
was going on under their lights & their solar
or sonar myopic microscopes >

or perhaps they had come to our boat specially
or especially to do this - we shall nvr know now that I
am awake from the dream - or perhaps I had heard of
them or heard from them or heard somehow that they
were conducting these tests or thests based on some
preconceived table or bed or menstrual thesis - & had
mentioned my 'problem' to Garath or one of the guys
on our boat - don't know why - perhaps because of what that cool
rulin night-nurse had tell me ? - but right away. as if. as I say
. they had really come to do just that >

as if we were under surveillance or a glass-bottom boat
or something like that > these guys
started asking questions & mmurmmuring these

thests as they call them. on

Garath & on me - bblood swabs rabies syringes icicle
needles sticky black blood-pressure cages & armbands
even urines ureas & ECGs pads cush. ites stings green
faced masks & thugs like that - it was a wonder what
they had on board that white hospital love boat
& terrific scientific battleship of law - & all this was
interesting because not only did they behave

but it seem by then that Garath & me had become mwe
or something dream siam
-ese like that. so that we were like feeling the same/thing
together & at the same/time slam as it were

so that we begin telling them about the mist un
-der our eyes like we was both wanting & hopin for a cure
w/out telling them - you know how it is - the full origin & nature
of the disease or problem we had. tho we very well knew what it > was
which surprise me a likkle. since until
that moment. when I suppose I recognize Garath - I at least certainly
didn't know or didn't know w/ such ceratainty >
but were hiding it. not only because we were awkward. like small/boys
wd have been at that time . & natural liars ditto. but it was

like some kind of 

like Ben Jonson perhaps. w/ his plays & his 'performance enhansing
stereos' . knowing full well that what he was doing was not 'right'

but arguing successfully to his twin & opposite (i.e to me or rather mwe)
that was it . when in the end - at the tape or bottomline
of the song - it was his

.

that muttered & that if he was not that. then nothing else matter
-ed & he wd be &/or remain a nobody & that it was better
to be caught trying to be somebody than be or remain innocent

&lean&

body ok? for who in the world cd over

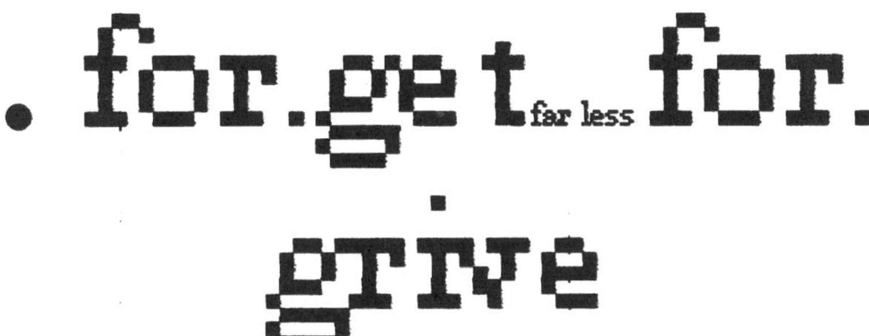

him if they nvr know him or of him in the first plate

And it was like that w/ Garath & mwe

We wanted them to find out - if they found out - since if
they found out it wd or might help w/ the cure. if there
was a cure. that is. but when all was said & done

we were hoping that they wd give us something to
elevate the mist & help or let us carry on doing what we
had always been doing & not interfere in any way w/
our care-free free-fare-ing days out in the sun & water.
is only when

the tests started. w/ all that paran**oil**ia on the high

seas that i have spoken about. that we realized how
serious & complex the problem was

the first diagnosis was that Garath & we was suffering
from some kind of allegory 'in
-duce (d) from **prolonged xplosure to the elements**'
- the sun & sea & the movement of watercoconuts
& the influence of salt . somehow. and the fish
that we had been eating

but the bad news. which they had not yet come to
. tho i think they knew it or were coming to
it w/ their inevitable machines

but this we didn't kno
tho I guess Garath had somehow dived or divine(d)
it - tho somehow I didn't this time

but Gararth I realize now. knew
what was going on what was coming & what it meant
&
didn't like it or want to have or hear
it

tho for one moment I sensed. before he close me out
. that he was *relieve* that at last somebody was
getting to his problem & secret

& that this. if not being or bringing a cure or crowd
wd or might bring him home peace - at least perhaps
for the price of some time

- & that the tablets that he had been talking all the time
- for whatever lesion - perhaps even he himself cdnt have told you
- and at first I had thought. when we were twins
. that they were like same sort of

medication - small thick

orange-coloured tetrahedrons in a paper
package w/(the tabloids I mean)
like a drift or gutter down the 'front' so that you cd
break or cut them plix into two - like what I saw
Granfather take for 'sugar' & 'pressure'
& 'night-blind-nesses' & 'nature' & things like
that so that he wd wake
up two tree sometimes four off-beat stanzas of the night
'to pass water' as he call it

& walk round 'checking the house' or more usually
just standin there in the country cane field darkness be
cause he was really waking in his sleep & couldn't walk
his way back home to his blood

but after Gararth 'left'. as it were. I realize that his tara-
gets were not like my grandfathers' or for those kind ->
those kind of mammal purposes at all
but that he was on

/whatever else that
meant. and that that must have been responsible
in some way for that mildew or milt/age
behind our eyes <

tho you well realize that he had been able to
successfully block all this off from me *even from mwe*

so that now. as I write. I can only half-sense what was
going on w/ him w/in him among his lakes & forests
along the tubes & starfish & undercurries of his ocean <
but I can tell you that as soon as he got to know
or sense what Randy & his scientists were tuning
up with >

(he had started calling them 'our white Muses or musicians' meaning magicians
since about

half post six

of the dreamon)

how they wd want or xpect him to go wash ashore to th (e) clinic or the White House or some other even more wilder lavoratory for

'more rigorous thests'

more stripping. that is. of his sacreds - the roses of butt er & fat curled up in his lobotomy despite all this salt >> waves. flyingfish hangovers & hang-ups in the halyard -

he suddenly cut out

& we find ourselves like on the back or belly of his big black wide-bellly bourgeon or barge like in

speeding away to the north away from where the scient-
ists had moor(ed) nxt to us for several quiet days & it <
was as if we were galloping upon the water & that the <
boat had become like some kind of four-headed chariot
& horse on which there was all this shooting & laught-
er & holiday-like be-

haviour like hostages on the

Jolly

Roger

& we know that the scientists w/Randy among them <<
were like in hot pursuit w/ their clarinets & sausages &
the dogs of their hearing-aids playing pizzicato in the >>
sails inside the control-station of the bridge of sound &
sometimes I was like on board Garath's boat &sometim-
es I was like w/ my old friend Bebe in his shop or laun-
ch so that I knew from time to time what the scientists >
were thinking & it wasn't a nice feeling or picture for it
seems that they had discovered. as he - & you - must >>

have already guess - I mean you have only to observe the foam & fall-out on this story - that my brother was becoming - more likely was - already was - in very grave danger of becoming some

kind of

DEREGULATION

or street

person or parason or pirate of the highway seas who depended for his kicks on certain at first hallucinatory acids & leaks to be got from hashes or squid or seamoss or fish & even shaegoe & rock-crab . which is why he had become like addicted to the boat & open sea & the creaks & washes of our shoreline & our hidden choral half-moon beaches. & they were saying that the tabloids he was talkin were like doin the same thing corrosive to hi-(m) like writing from the

inside & that if he didn't stop -

which was probably too late now - there were already too many lobsters & crayfish in the slop-pans or some-thing like that

& that ~~*if he wasn't stopp(ed)*~~-
& that was the point - tho some of them thought that it was already too late

even for 

that the double combination of these trays wd
completely erode some wall or hall or well
of understanding in his brain or belly -

in his BODY

& that he wd become - if he was not that already. some
of them were saying on their boat - a full-blown full-
bodied sea -

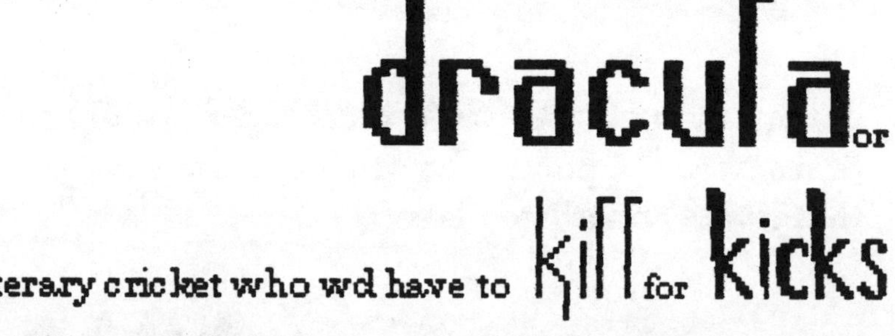
dracula or
literary cricket who wd have to kill for kicks

which. they said. is what had made him take off
in the first place
- because he was already made - he was already mad
- & had heard that there was probably no cure

for his cold
- so why then shd he hang around & be their poisoner
when they wd be able to do nothing but wash him off
w/Liberal or Christian or Scientific kindness
& that he preferr
-ed to take his chances riding the watery wastes off
the cool orisha shores of our island as he had
always done

& who knows but that whatever was wrong
might not eventually submerge or subside or
just go away

& if not he wd at least be controlling his own history
& progression as he had always wanted to do
& had in fact started to do

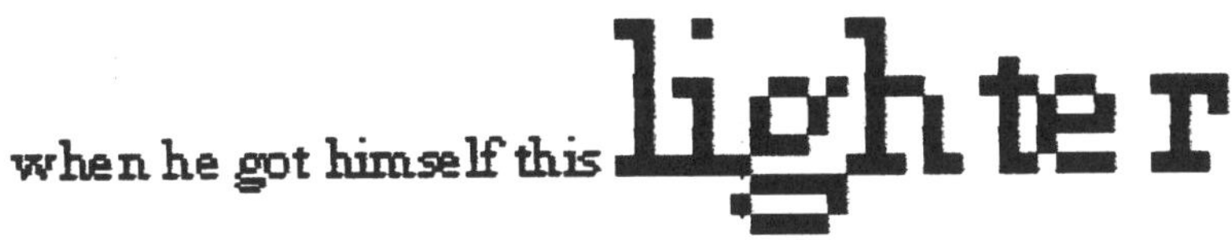
when he got himself this lighter

PART TWO

The lighter speed south of man

-kind for days w/ the stereophonic farmers
& pharmacists in hot & confident pursuit

making planes & analyses. perdicting our route. where we might
step. where we might stop. our options. when & where we might
run out of gears or gas. as General Swartzkorff's men must have
done to the Iroquois in Operation Bootstrap or Bootstorom
in 1991

but Days & Nights pass & Days & Nights pass
& we were still pissing into the tears of the wind/ward nicely
ahead of the scientists until at last we approached Speightstown
& there was like this bridge

but really long jetty out in the anchor  jutt

-ing out into our path w/a red wooden boom
& is here that the Americans had perdicted - *yes!*
- that we wd stop or be stopped if we went that way
but I saw Garath's horse like leap up out of the water & over
that bridge & barrier & the boat came back down w/ a bang
on

the other side still making white water & travelling on across the
labour or harbour w/our stunning Iraqui hostages rocking from
side to side & half-stemmed from the leap into space & the speed

and looking back we cd see the US scientists in their white green
yacht or lunch frustrated at the low bright bridge or barrier
of the day & like a cheer went up in our boat that we had escalp
(ed) from them & were now headed out to sea
& curving south around the island

when for the first time I witness
what a monster my brother Garath had so suddenly be
-come as if a plug had been pulled out of our boat

& it had quickly filled w/wonder & was sinking into the sun
of the sea but the opposite of this if you see what I mean

-vva since our escape . as I say. he was li-
ke very much in the ascendant but his elation & hunger had now
es. calated to ranting & raving like the huge

at the beginning of this sentence out here in the bough up front
in the pew like a lookout or Ahab or Viking where before he wd
have been grinning & gentle & easy even when the waves banged
the prow like a prayer & lifted it up. flinging it out into the rain .
he holding on to a rope. one looped to a cleat or a ring which swi
vell w/him as the boat gallop & surge & he was like guiding our
progress from here in the bough even though he is now so distant
from us - *capitain* - but nvr now one of the crew - the man at the

helm w/a prob **helm** they

say and there was like this floatin slag or stage or deck
or as it turned out

death-buoy

out in the sea.. a kind of look-out or perhaps research platform
as if we were prospecting for evil or oil or gold off the cost
of Barabados tho it probably had more to do w/ our Govt's
at last interest in deep sea marine diving & divining & research
esp fish & there was this only guy on board on the tilting & heav
ing & hot naked platform in the afternoon silver & I can't tell
you anything other than that it was a guy who was just sitting
there & I don't know if he was smoking or just '*considering*' or
fishing or just tilling the ocean w/ his eyes - how it moved
& glistened & was like some great quilt or skin & perhaps
glittering tremendous **feel** & he was safe from it - felt safe from it
- who knows - tho he might have been frighten or llobbllolly out
there & might have been looking out to sea
where there was nothing to see really

-cept perhaps lonely or guilty or a cloud bank of n'uit on
the horizon or a squail or a sudden squall like a headache or
migraine

or

the low cry of a black Amerindian seabird its beak watching
its squaw face just under the dark water
or he might have aben loking in the direction
of our drunken island & might have seen it from time to time tho

most of the time

esp from his being so low in the water & such a distance out in
the prairies
it wd have been invisible like below the horizon

but some

-times I know it wd have come tilting up even if leaf
for a moment like how milk spills up for a monet from a moving
cup if you see what I mean

tho of course it wouldnt have been like that at all out there
in the salt milkless

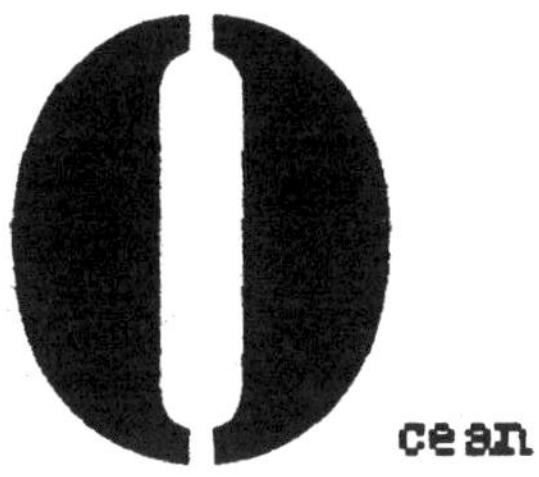

cean

starsight at this guy & the platform/on the platform
& he was shouting something into the wind
as we came at something like 10 to 15 killerwatts

& was waving his left hand like in a clutching motion

as if he was yelling the guy out of the forum even tho he was
standing on

. shall we say. an immovable object or rock & there was no
way that he cd get out of the way unless he took off & dive
into the sea which he didn't do

& Garath

was like clutching at him thru the aria
as if practising something like singing or slow bowling &
as I say yelling out all the time as our boat approached that
floating flatform of fear at this white terrific speed w/out slowing

down & like in slow mo
-tion now as we sloshed alongside just swerving in time &still
going straight on w/our journey to nowhere w/out slowing down
our clanking & engines & the sound of water & wind in our ears

the salt on our skin & the dazzle of eyelash in the hot afternoon
in almost sight of belov: ed Barbadoes where all of us. even
the guy on the platform. I am sure. had been born & bleed
& I saw. as I say. as if in slow motion. my brother. still yelling
. stretch out the crow of his hand like just ahead of my belief
& forboding at this guy in the dock as if he was de
-manding - as we came up close close close alongside - wd you be
-lieve it! - his

of all things - so that the guy must have been like helpless
& naked though I didn't notice any of this at the time
.but he must have been or aben naked for what
happen to happen
- & the guy was like shouting back

at Gareth
-
& his great clutching fingers that gripp. as we
pass. into this poor man's loins. his sticky red fingers down into
the nest of the man's heirs. whether thick or not didn't matter
. & warp his hand round his wally as if it was a kind of towline or
sail or rail rope & then curl his hand round it like tie

-ing a **knot** - a bowline or granny or reef knot

&pull w/the great real power of our boat taking everything along
w/it while we watched in like a great bowl
or howl
as his hand wremch&

pull &the guy's cock was out from the

roots

hi-jack through the air as our boat speed away in Gar's
pulmonary hands & it was like
balack & squirming. or perhaps I imagine that it shd have been
like this but we cd see it > the clear sky for a moment as Gareth's
hand came round from the platform
back to our boat in a wide arc thru the air
to his head thrown back *for Chris-sake* and w/the boat
panting again & like shivering through the water as we resume
our curse

i&i watch the man who had been my twin & other bring
that cock to the gate of his mouth to his thief & I watch him bite
it like in half

like a small snake or shrimp or a fife of sound
& swallow the fat red bleeding part of it nearest to him
- **like the guy's protean shoots was**

what he was after - & toss-way the head the way you wd toss
-way a dead eel or fish-head into the sea among still floating
silverblue fishscales & melts w/out losing speed w/out looking
back/down still hanging on to that - to that root & rope
of the bow-line as if nothing
had happen & we went on for several Days & Nights
- *yes* - more like this w/out stoopping or stripping
or losing speed towards the

of the island

& I watch him do the same to three or four of our hostages
leaving them bleeding & dead w/white staring
eyes ticking yellow in the salt under the wooden wet cross
-benches in the bilge & thwart of the vessel & the black absent

holes between their generations & their heels like tucked up
under them & each time he wd just sit up here in the bough
of himself as if he was encase - I remember
noticing this even during the dream
- in like a sleeve of air & silence & he gave his whole demeanour
. *for that is the word that came flying to me like a sea-bird*
a kind of *frigate* of **weight** or

garavity

tho all we cd see was the slight slump of his back. his two ears sticking out of the bark of his head like the sound of bats & the bent & naked & vulnerable nape of his neck & what must have been the red salt-pitted pittiless struggle w/him

PART THREE

hen we at last reach the South

there was like this **Wall** of salvages which must have been but there years & years before in the days when there were Tourists perhaps. to keep out barracuda or sharks or DNA/mutations of DNA which stop us now from going any further > so that our boat cut its engines & we threw some tyres over the side to stop it from scraping its sides or smashing itself on the wall & we drifted there up against that wall for a long time several Days & Nights it seems. but w/ no sense of worry in our moorings since Garth or Gareth knew that we had

ARRIVED

that there was no/where else to go to. to hide to. to run to. to run
from. & so we relax & enjoyed the light & the sheen & foam of
the water & the peace
of the silence as if we were on holiday & were playing whist
or **warri**

tho nobody had said anything to anybody else
ever since Gareth's first killing so that our boat which in the 'old
days' had been like a sea-horse out of the water was now lapped
like a hearse. if you kno what
i mean. tho as i say we were happy

until young Robin Breeze
came on broad after the fourth day & in the meantime Gareth
kept like unto himself like into himself. half-finished & half-
naked in his shorts & his two naked ears w/ their bats to us. like
because he nvr now made face w/ us or lett
the young eyes that the Lord
had given him it seemed a long long while ago now. make four
make four
w/ us w/ ours & so he dived ate fish & squid through these long
sunlit summit

Days

& Nights reflecting in our sunbit 

tho sometimes we see him like cooking up in what was now the
great dark jaws of the bow & smoking. and he seem yes
quite content in this distant shelf of himself
after the orbit of the storm

Part Four

When Robin arrive - altho he shd have been almost 60

since I had lost seen him as a sea-cub inna the Royal Bubbados Sea Scouts - he was as young as ever as if no jellies or sea-moss had come oshuun ashore year after year after year as if nothing had happen & he had not left the Barabajan Spiders to become a puisne judge in Ber. muda or was it Bahamas -

so he was as young & fresh & breezy & innocent as he had ever been when he used to ride bicycle & looked like his sister & he < must have come out from the mainland or from some nearby atoll or island in a skiff or corial

but I suddenly see him on the seawall - I recall it well because < before I see him I had been looking for a long time at a wet shae-goe that cling to the sharp pitted rock of the wall each time a wave came up & it had close its eyes - flatten them into its flat shell that is - & *press* itself down into its brief purchase of sweat & was still there wet & jewell each time after the wave had wash-by & I think that I or rather Gareth

or Gawth

must have been thinking of eating it even tho shaegoes seem so lacking in any acrid or juice that we cd use even in our dry hung er & thirst & we knew that some of them were well prisoned/-impoisoned as they were in their hard inscape carapace -

it was then

like I say. that Robim is here & he came on board - didn't need no wode or invitation from us - wdn't have asked for one neither - wdnt have xpected any -

& began chatting w/ Gareth as if nothing had happened But he also brought the news

that the Muses were still following following & that they wd reach where we were at the Wall in a few days & he asked Garth laughing what was he going to do about it &

Gawth or Gareth laugh back & dived over the side & came up blowing water like in the old days & splashing happily like on holiday & said

nothing
- he was so unconcerted -

which was fair enough & typical
of Gareth or Garth & true to his 'principles' to his
kind of folk 'music'
since he had now done all he cd do - got as far as

the **Wall** & now

there was nothing more

he cd do but enjoy - *butterflies* - this like - so mwe had been right

about this all along

holiday

So he & Robin splash in the>

water & talk for like days on end & mad plenty fumm & joke(s) w/each other as if nothing had happen until the morning Robim ask him about the

>> word he use -

& it so happen
that Garth. only a short while before. while Robim I think was st ill asleep or had gone off into the past of his skiff or something >> like that - had had like what was to be his last 'one' the last 'host-age' left in our

bloat

after that it wd have been Robim & mwe - & when Robim come back or wake up & cd see what had happen or cd guess anyway from all the blood & the dead body & the

agitation

tho he didn't show any change of face or even heart - xpressed no surprise or alarm - since I suppose he was part of the dream. xcept that he became quite quiet & like subdued & he was like this for a long time before he asked Gareth the

Question

& I remember him not answearing at first. but not because he didn't want to but more because like he didn't overstand what Robim was asking - as I soon realized -

he had
come to

penises

for granted

& must have assume that everybody eat them
like fish. I suppose. & so it was no big ting. havin(g) lost contact
utterly. it seems. w/ his

>> conscience <<

until something make him
recognize that Robim was serious & really wanted to know

& it was then that Robim seem to have reach
& touch him. deep down there in that fire
still burning inside him like in that tree we were speaking about
earlier

something that I had wish all these days
that I wd have had the good strength or fortune to have done for
my friend but couldn't

because I guess I was too slippit & divided myself &
contaminated & weak & dishonest - like the very opposite of
Robim really - so that in a way - & I am able to say this now

which I suppose is an advance or at least I hope it is - that is mwe
as much as anybody if not anything that is responsible for what
happen to Gareth & I first come to see this when I see him really
beginning to listen to what Robim was askin & I cd sense -

really **sense** him again as if we were saman again - that he really no longer know what **cock** was. but saw it simply as fish as I've said or a square rut of food & he told Robim this & as if to prove it. now devil or serpent or fallin god. he slipp overboard & return w/ the head of Mr S'S cock that had been floating slowly down-> wards in the water, like a soft mangrove stump . dead druid man-a-war by the shaegoe & the

Wall

& he went down & like dive it up since it had not yet reach the > blottom & the water was clear & he was xpert enough to remember roughly when he had bitten it off & throw(n)

it overboard & the rate at which it must have been sinking & in > which direction it was slinking (you see I knew now that this is how he see it) & so he brought it back up on the first try in the plan of him hann li ke how we bring up coins or sea-egg or sea-plate or even snails < or starfish or sometimes difficult sea-roaches or migrating unprotested conches embedding in the sand

he had scoop it up. that little black tube
in the water
. bobbin about on its own like it was lost
. which it was

& he hell it up in his hand as he surface
. his head & hand in the sum
-light & ask

Robim

& throw it into the boat in the same/ way that we throw sea-eggs or jackfish or sea-cats & millet from our fish-pots

& then he swim back to the box that our boat had become . kick ed - pushing himself up out of the water & grabbing a side of the coffin -

haul himself up

the side. high up as he cd kick himself up from the slack thick & the pull of his hands. so that as he come upwards against the sm-ooth gunwale & throw his body upward &

over it. flip-kicking one last time as he was coming up out of the white noise of the water

& w/his body now over the gunwale. pressing onto & over it har (d) w/ his hands so that his hips & his waist cork-screwed under him so that he was up & out of the twist & sat on the gunwale w/ his hands to his face punishing the water out of his eyes & like >> resting a moment all wet & streaming & mirrow w/water. blowin (g) it out of his noise & shaking his head to unclugg it out of his > ears & feeling then. I shd think. his youth & his strength & his sl- imness & his cock & his balls all tight & safe in his soaking wet > swimming-suit against the warm brown brow of the wood of the gunwale & he turn(ed) where he was & took up the dead-leff & twig. really. of Mr Stimm's *manhood* from out of the soft slem wor- (m)wood hiss of the water under the row-boards & turned it over in his hands now drying in the sunlight & wind w/the waves sud- denly whipping up white like all over the page of the sea. like am- persands & turned it over&over again & said nothing for like a > long time. like he was considering what he really had there. the valve & value & enigma. & the now black broeken animal flower of it etc etc etc

& then he say to Robin that it is a penis as if we didn't know that as if we didn't know that and as if we didn't know what had happ en to it & for him to have done what he had so horribly wrung w/ out knowing -

- see what I mean? -

as if he hadn't just a short while ago torn it out currt from inside Mr Stimpson's blue victim bathsuit & pants & bitten half of it off & swallowed it whole. throwing the little cockle & head of its gr- istle away as he had done all the others

And is then that round
the bend of the sandbank come Randy
Burkenheit & the US science monitors w/soft
music from their bow-wave
already reaching us in clear liquid quavers
before they arrive

as Gareth sleep overboard & went down deep to the very
roots of the sea-

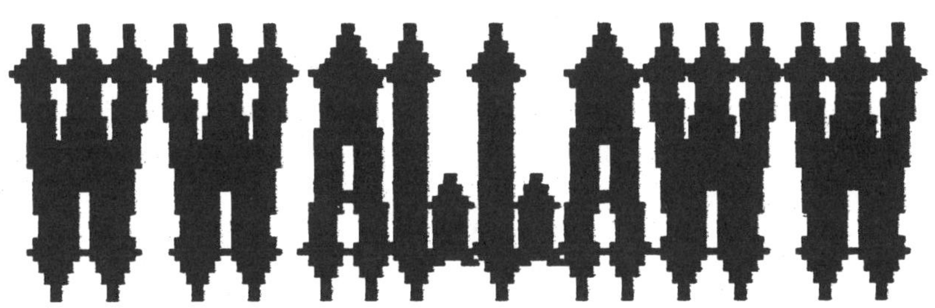

as I know he wd & that he must have been struggling to find
down
down
down
down
under there some insect of incest

or

china or berlim or eyeless palestrinian

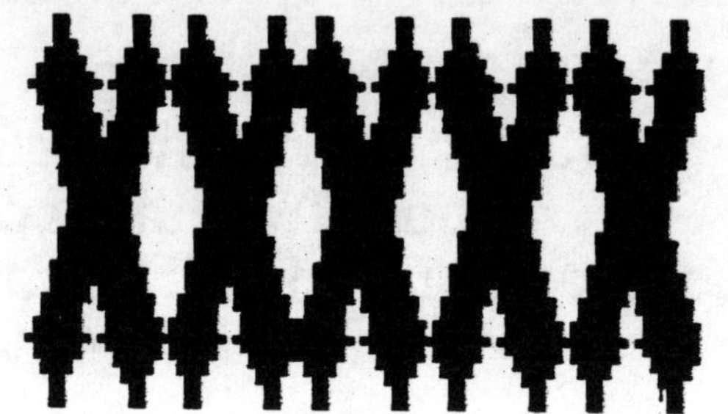

or 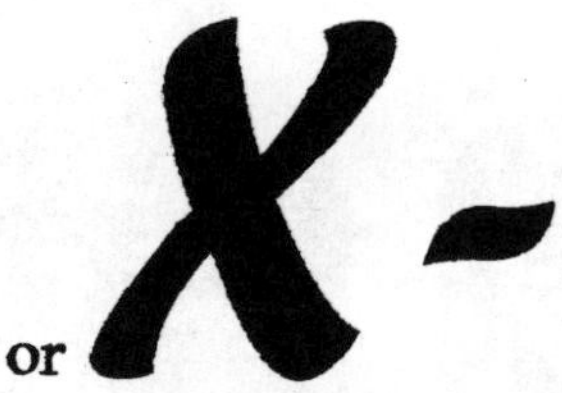

it that we knew wasn't there but still hope there might be
& more & more des. perately try
-ing to find the breath
to go down & stay
down as he trie to embrace what chains & tendrils
& entanglements he cd fine down there near
the trinkets
& irie sea-roses of Vasco da Gama
& settelling seines & the sea
-noises that appear onm his tomb
on the righthand side of the sun of his brain
w/its ribbons & shadows

lost sparks specks embers metastases eyes eyelids irises of
light fire
-flies of sun
-set floating up from the dark & his dreaming
of beaches w/the lost
sound of sand drifting into the forests
of feather
-less future
-less fish
scaleless birds coral white scavenger flesh
on the boughs & the boulders
of the dark green i
:ron of seaweed

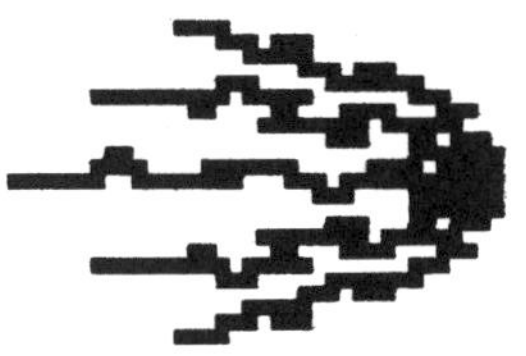

-em-
fetterments of clear air become water beyond
his mutation. dissolving
into this tinkle & oven
of silence. Musa. dead arawaks
drown sailors drown steersmen
my brothers drown fishermen drown
Dahomean slaves
w/no glint or dream in their fishernets
that cd not stop the tide

while up above
in the land
of the living
where the water is

weir & the glitter=
ing sloop
of musicians come
slowly
around in a sweet
liquid loop of
crystal alongside the
war & wharf of our
derelict lighter &
take Mr Stimmon's

now gutted-out hulk
in a dinghy
& hose-down the
blood
& scales from our
musgrave
w/ something like
bleach
& jeyes fluid

& waited around
searching every
watery corner & tune
of the place dredging
for - Gareth -
foam ripple tell-tale
bugles of ash &
wreath of wireless
sea-breathings

the

STARS & STRIPS

flapping for-
ever it seem
in the late afternoon
coffle & traffic
of depth-flares
& fllowers of divers
-un-
till it started to late

the growing
impatience of
searching for
searching for
searching forGareth
forGareth
forGareth
forGareth

the air & the water
w/the evening light
now chilly upon it &
blowing
across to the pale
fading stripes
of the beaches
not a footprint in
sight

on their smooth
reaches. and I seem
to recall it must have
been Randy turn-
ing to me as if I was
Gareth or if I was not
as if Gareth as
Gareth was no
longer here

as if Garath
had not or had nvr
been here was no
longer my twin or
my brother or my
soso intimate enemy
& insouciant other
& frenn &
I remember I
say Burkenhead
turning to me in that

sea-island sea-light
w/the waves by the

SeaWall

coming quietly in as the
evening come down on
the darking salvages &

saying

to me that they going ashore for
the while of a drink or a cuppa a
cocoa or be da da cola & wdn't I
like to come along now

● ● ●

or join them later

● ● ●

Kingston May 1991 rev Aug 1993 . pub DS (1994) . rev + restructure for NO June, July 2003
to Sunday 27 July 03 w/lots of hard hungry unxpected solo coumbite
NYC 7 Nov 05